Even *More* **House Specialties**

Created by Deanna House

Book Design by Craig Minor

Illustrations by Pamela Myhre

Enjoy! Enjoy!
Deanna House

Copyright © 1992
House Specialties
P.O. Box 242
Ada, Michigan 49301

15,000 copies in print

Published by Deanna House Specialties, Inc.
Library of Congress Catalogue Card Number 92-074856
ISBN # 0-9610752-2-8

About the Author

DEANNA HOUSE

Photo: David H. Curl

"Enthusiastic teaching makes learning fun" continues to be one of Deanna House's favorite mottos. Whether she is teaching an adult education class, presenting a workshop for 4-H members or speaking to community groups, she shares her positive living philosophy as she communicates through food.

Deanna is a graduate of University of Wisconsin-Stout and has taught junior high, senior high and adult home economics education classes. She is a free lance food writer regularly read in the Kalamazoo Gazette and The Grand Rapids Press.

A native of rural southern Wisconsin, Deanna has spent most of her adult life in southwest Michigan. After living in Portage, Michigan for nineteen years, she and her husband, George, now live in Ada near Grand Rapids. They are the parents of two adult children, Paul, a Chemist, and Sara, a Special Education teacher.

Her professional affiliations include membership in the American Home Economics Association, Michigan Home Economics Association, International Microwave Power Institute Cooking Appliance Section, National Press Women and Michigan Press Women.

About the Designer

Craig Minor, Graphic Designer is responsible for the design of this book as well as its' companions, *House Specialties* and *More House Specialties*. He is a Kalamazoo, Michigan native with a BFA from Western Michigan University and an MFA from Cranbrook Academy of Art. Craig currently resides in Houston, Texas with his wife Stephanie and son Christopher. He is principal of Minor Design Group, Inc., Director of the Graphic Design Program at the University of Houston and president of the Texas chapter of the American Institute of Graphic Arts.

Prelude

Hello Cooking Friend,

Welcome to Even More House Specialties, the third member of an exciting family of cookbooks designed to share well tested recipes from my house to your house.

Within these pages you'll find an array of new recipes that follow the familiar House Specialties format. Most of the ideas use everyday ingredients complete with easy step-by-step directions that produce mouth watering results.

Approximately one third of the recipes in this collection feature the timely attributes of cooking with less fat, salt, and/or sugar. Watch for this symbol:

This apple with a heart helps to identify those recipes that especially promote healthy eating habits.

It has been a humbling, heartwarming experience to realize that many folks have cooked extensively from the first two House Specialties cookbooks. So it is my hope that this new interesting variety of recipes will also provide you hours of cooking pleasure.

As with most sizeable projects, cookbook writing is not a one person task. From sharing with me the House family name to his loving encouragement and support, including his financial expertise and proof reading skills, my husband, George, has played an integral part in this effort.

Special thanks to Craig Minor, graphic designer extraordinaire, whose talent and expertise have guided me now through three creative cookbooks.

Much appreciation goes to my special friend, Mary Ellen Behm, who spent hours proof reading this collection, her third cookbook assisting endeavor. Thanks also to my friend, Mary Koenig, and our daughter, Sara, for proof reading sessions.

It is my sincere wish that many of these simply significant recipes will become favorites of your family and friends.

Happy Cooking.

Deanna House

Contents

Cooking with less Recipes highlighted by this symbol contain less fat, less salt or less sugar.

Microwave Cooks: The microwave directions in this book are for use with units having 600-700 watts. If oven with lower wattage is used microwave cooking times need to be increased.

Tasty Beginnings

Let's begin this collection of significant recipes with a selection of cold and hot appetizers as well as a grouping of cold and hot beverages.

From the great flavor of homemade salsa to an interesting potato skin idea, many of these recipes keep in mind the wholesome philosophy of "Cooking Light".

Refreshing beverages are mandatory when it comes to fully enjoying appetizers and snacks, so here is a first class offering of fruit based punch recipes.

Contents

GREAT SALSA

[Makes 2½ cups]

As salsa gains in popularity, it is fast becoming a staple item in lots of households. So now is the time to explore salsa making yourself. This dynamite recipe is a great way to begin.

1 **[28 ounce] can "seasoned" diced tomatoes or whole tomatoes, chopped, or 2 large peeled chopped fresh tomatoes**
1 **[4 ounce] can chopped green chilies, mild, medium or hot**
½ **cup thinly sliced green onions**
1 **teaspoon grated lemon peel**
¼ **teaspoon salt**
½ **teaspoon oregano leaves**
⅛ **teaspoon ground pepper**
2 **tablespoons lemon juice**

1. Drain tomatoes, saving juice for another use.
2. In large bowl, combine drained tomatoes, chilies, green onions, lemon peel, salt, oregano, pepper and lemon juice.
3. Mix well.
4. Cover; refrigerate several hours to blend flavors.
5. Serve with Tortilla Chips made from the folowing recipe, if desired.

TORTILLA CHIPS

[Makes 96 chips]

These crispy snacks have approximately half as many fat grams as their purchased counterpart. Top that off with great flavor and you have two reasons to get into the chip making business.

12 [8-10 inch] flour tortillas

1. Cut each tortilla into 8 wedges. [I find a kitchen scissors works very well.]
2. Place wedges in single layer on ungreased cookie sheet.
3. Bake in preheated 350 degree oven 10-15 minutes or until light golden brown.
4. Serve with salsa.

Tuna Pecan Pate

[Makes 2¼ cups]

This tasty tuna spread can quickly be mixed together in a food processor, or the ingredients can be chopped individually and blended evenly with softened cream cheese and seasonings by hand. Serve as an appetizer or take to a tail gate gathering.

¼ **cup chopped fresh parsley**
1 **medium onion, finely chopped**
1 **cup chopped pecans**
1 **[8 ounce] package light or regular cream cheese, softened**
1 **[6 and ½ ounce] can tuna, drained, flaked**
½ **teaspoon salt**
Few dashes hot pepper sauce

1. In food processor bowl or mixing bowl, combine parsley, onion and pecans. Pulse or toss to blend.

2. Add cream cheese, tuna, salt and hot pepper sauce. Mix well.

3. Cover; refrigerate. Garnish and serve with crackers.

Layered Shrimp Appetizer

[Serves 8-10]

I've often watched friends gather together and completely devour this easy-to-create appetizer. To me, that's proof enough to make this recipe again and again.

1 **[8 ounce] package light or regular cream cheese, softened**
1 **tablespoon milk**
¾ **cup cocktail sauce**
6-8 **ounces frozen cooked shrimp, thawed**
½ **cup chopped, seeded cucumber**
3 **tablespoons sliced green onion, including tops**

1. In small bowl, combine cream cheese and milk; beat until smooth and fluffy.

2. Spread cream cheese mixture over bottom of 10-inch round attractive serving plate.

3. Spread cocktail sauce evenly over cream cheese mixture.

4. Top with shrimp, cucumber and onions.

5. Refrigerate until serving time. Serve with assorted crackers

Turkey Salad Appetizers

[Makes 24-30 appetizers]

Slices of crisp cucumber provide the perfect base for these appealing appetizer bites. Add a small amount of tasty turkey salad, garnished with pimiento, and you have an attractive tasty beginning.

¾   cup finely chopped, cooked turkey
⅓   cup finely chopped celery
2   tablespoons chopped pimiento, drained
2   tablespoons light or regular mayonnaise or salad dressing
     Dash of salt, if desired
     Dash of pepper
1   medium cucumber

1. If available, use a food processor to chop the turkey.

2. In small mixing bowl, combine turkey, celery, pimiento, mayonnaise, salt and pepper. Mix well. Cover and chill.

3. Cut cucumber into ¼ inch thick slices.

4. Spoon one rounded teaspoonful on each cucumber slice.

5. Garnish with additional pimiento.

Corned Beef Spirals

[Makes 60 appetizers]

People who work at the Deli counter of your favorite super market will gladly slice corned beef 1/8 inch thick for this quick and easy appetizer. Busy cooks will be happy to know these tiny snacks can be made up to 24 hours before serving time.

½   pound corned beef, sliced ⅛ inch thick
¼   cup olive and pimiento flavored soft cream cheese

1. Spread each corned beef slice with cream cheese; roll up tightly. Wrap in plastic wrap.

2. Refrigerate at least 2 hours.

3. With sharp knife, cut into ½ inch pieces.

4. Serve with frilly toothpicks.

SOUTH OF THE BORDER SNACKING SQUARES

[Makes 4-5 dozen squares]

Here is a clever colorful way to serve the ever popular layered Mexican appetizer. Tender refrigerated crescent rolls create an ideal base for this crowd pleasing recipe. It's both easy to serve and devour.

2   **[8 ounce] cans refrigerated quick crescent dinner rolls**
1   **[16 ounce] can refried beans**
1   **cup light or regular sour cream [8 ounces]**
2   **tablespoons taco seasoning mix [from 1 & 1/4 oz. package]**
1½ **cups shredded Cheddar cheese [6 ounces]**
¼   **cup sliced green onions**
½   **cup chopped green bell pepper**
1   **cup chopped, seeded tomatoes**
½   **cup sliced ripe olives**

1. Unroll dough into 4 long rectangles.

2. Place crosswise in ungreased 10x15 inch jellyroll pan; press over bottom and 1-inch up sides to form crust.

3. Firmly press perforations to seal.

4. Bake in preheated 375 degree oven 15-20 minutes or until golden brown. Cool completely.

5. Spread beans over crust.

6. In small bowl, combine sour cream and taco seasoning mix; mix well.

7. Spread sour cream mixture over beans.

8. Sprinkle cheese, onion, green pepper, tomatoes and olives evenly over sour cream.

9. Cover; refrigerate an hour to blend flavors.

10. Cut into squares.

Spinach Vegetable Dip

[Makes 3 cups]

Lowfat yogurt is a great heart smart base for this popular vegetable dip. It's a perfect partner for making a big dip in fat, cholesterol and calories.

2   **cups lowfat yogurt**
1   **[10 ounce] package frozen chopped spinach, thawed, drained and squeezed dry**
⅓   **cup minced fresh onion**
1   **[8 ounce] can water chestnuts, drained and chopped**
1   **[0.9 ounce] envelope dry vegetable soup mix**
    Assorted raw vegetables for dipping

1. Drain off any excess liquid from yogurt.
2. In medium mixing bowl, combine yogurt, spinach, onion, water chestnuts and dry vegetable soup mix.
3. Mix well to thoroughly combine ingredients.
4. Cover and refrigerate at least 2 hours before serving.
5. Serve as a dip for raw vegetables.

Mexican Encore

[Serves 8-10]

You'll know where this appetizer gets its name when you watch guests return again and again to dip tortilla chips in this layered specialty. It's a popular poolside snack or tailgate treat.

1   **[8 ounce] package light or regular cream cheese, softened**
2   **large ripe avocados, peeled, seeded and cut into chunks**
1   **teaspoon seasoned salt**
1   **cup picante or thick salsa sauce, mild, medium or hot**
1   **cup finely shredded lettuce**
1   **medium tomato, seeded and diced**
½   **cup sliced ripe olives**
¼   **cup sliced green onions with tops**
1   **cup shredded sharp Cheddar cheese**
    Regular and/or blue tortilla chips

[continued]

Mexican Encore [continued]

1. Combine cream cheese, avocados and salt in food processor or blender container. Process or blend until smooth, scraping down sides once or twice.

2. Spread mixture onto a 12 inch round platter forming a 10-inch circle with a rim.

3. Spoon picante or salsa sauce evenly over avocado mixture.

4. Top with lettuce, tomato, olives, onions and cheese.

5. Serve with assorted tortilla chips.

Marinated Melon Pick Ups

[Makes 12-16 appetizer servings]

Bite size treats, served on frilly toothpicks, are always an appealing way to tease the appetite. These citrus-flavored snacks are as quick and easy to prepare as they are to consume.

1	**medium cantaloupe melon**
1	**medium honey dew melon**
4	**ounces thinly sliced cooked ham**
48	**frilly toothpicks**
1	**cup orange juice**
¼	**cup lime juice**
2	**tablespoons honey**

1. Cut melons in half. Remove seeds and fibers from center of each.

2. Using melon baller, make about 24 balls from each melon.

3. Cut ham into 4x½ inch strips.

4. Wrap one ham strip around each melon ball; secure with cocktail pick.

5. In non-metal flat container, combine orange juice, lime juice and honey.

6. Place wrapped melon balls in orange juice mixture.

7. Cover; marinate in refrigerator at least 2 hours to blend flavors.

8. Drain melon balls; serve.

CREAMED HERRING AND ONIONS

[Serves 10-12]

Years ago, a gourmet friend shared with me his philosophy that adding sour cream to pickled herring produced a superior product. One bite of this creamed herring and I'm sure you'll agree.

1 **[22 ounce] jar pickled herring, drained, reserving liquid**
½ **cup light or regular sour cream**
½ **cup thinly sliced red onion, separated into rings**
¼ **cup chopped green onions**

1. In medium bowl, combine herring and sour cream; toss to coat. Cover; refrigerate.

2. In small glass bowl, combine red onion rings, green onions and reserved liquid from herring. Cover; refrigerate 1 or 2 hours.

3. Drain onions; discard liquid.

4. Add onions to herring mixture in medium bowl; toss to coat.

5. Refrigerate until serving time.

MOLDED CUCUMBER APPETIZER

[Makes 4½ cups]

Guests are coming for dinner. Lowfat is a dietary priority. You'd like to serve flavorful food with flair. Suggestion: Start with this interesting cucumber creation.

¼ **cup boiling water**
1 **envelope unflavored gelatin**
¼ **cup cold water**
2 **cups peeled, seeded, cut up cucumber**
1 **cup cut up celery**
1 **medium onion, quartered**
½ **large green pepper**
1 **cup lowfat cottage cheese**
½ **cup light mayonnaise**

1. In 1 cup glass measurer, dissolve gelatin in boiling water.

2. Add cold water.

[continued]

MOLDED CUCUMBER APPETIZER [continued]

3. In food processor, blender or by hand, coarsely chop cucumber, celery, onion and green pepper.

4. Remove vegetables to medium mixing bowl.

5. In processor bowl, blender container or with electric mixer, combine cottage cheese and mayonnaise. Process, blend, or beat until mixture is smooth.

6. Add cottage cheese mixture to vegetables.

7. Add gelatin to vegetables and mix thoroughly.

8. Pour into oiled 5-6 cup mold. Chill.

9. Unmold and garnish attractively.

10. Serve with assorted vegetables or lowfat crackers.

MINI RICE CAKE MORSELS

[Serves 6]

Mini rice cakes provide a perfect base for this picture pretty light appetizer. These bite size treats are so delicious they could actually double as dessert.

1   **cup vanilla yogurt**
¼   **cup drained juice packed crushed pineapple**
⅛   **teaspoon cinnamon**
24   **miniature honey-nut or other flavored rice cakes**
    Assorted cut up fruit like strawberries, blueberries,
    Mandarin orange segments, pineapple tidbits, etc.

1. About 24 hours before preparing this recipe, drain the yogurt to make ½ cup vanilla yogurt cheese using the directions on page 270.

2. In small mixing bowl, combine drained yogurt, crushed pineapple and cinnamon.

3. Spread teaspoonful of yogurt mixture over each rice cake; top with a piece or two of fruit.

4. Serve immediately.

CREAMY FRUIT DIP

[Makes 10-12 appetizer servings]

Even though fresh fruits are delicious when served alone, there are festive occasions when an interesting fruit dip is welcome. Healthy hearts will appreciate this lowfat version that's packed with outstanding flavor as well as good nutrition.

2 **cups vanilla yogurt**
¼ **cup frozen pineapple juice concentrate, thawed and undiluted**
2 **tablespoons honey**
2 **teaspoons poppy seeds**
   Fresh fruit such as strawberries, pineapple, oranges, apples, pears, etc.

1. About 24 hours before preparing this recipe, drain the yogurt to make 1 cup vanilla yogurt cheese using the directions on page 270.

2. In small mixing bowl, combine 1 cup vanilla yogurt cheese, pineapple juice concentrate, honey and poppy seeds.

3. Serve with an attractive selection of fresh fruit.

SAVORY SEASONED POPCORN

[Makes 10 cups]

Popcorn is a favorite snack for lots of folks, so it's no wonder this crunchy mixture is popular. By using butter-flavored cooking spray instead of butter or margarine, the fat content is lowered without loss of flavor.

8 **cups air-popped popcorn**
2 **cups miniature pretzels**
   Butter-flavored non-stick cooking spray
1 **teaspoon dried Italian seasoning, crushed**
¼ **teaspoon garlic powder**

1. In large bowl, combine popcorn and pretzels.

2. Stir gently while spraying mixture generously with non-stick cooking spray.

3. Immediately sprinkle with Italian seasoning and garlic powder; toss to coat well.

4. Store in tightly covered container.

DILLED VEGETABLE STICKS

[Serves 6-8]

Raw vegetables are commonplace when we plan appetizers and snacks. For a change of pace, do try these crisply cooked delicious dilled vegetables. Be prepared; you may be asked for the recipe.

2	**cups water**
¾	**cup vinegar**
½	**cup sugar**
1	**teaspoon salt**
1½	**tablespoons chopped fresh dillweed or 1 and ½ teaspoons dried dill weed**
1	**teaspoon onion powder**
¼	**teaspoon garlic powder**
½	**pound fresh whole green beans, tips removed**
3	**large carrots, cut into julienne strips**
3	**stalks celery, cut into julienne strips**

1. In large Dutch oven or saucepan, combine water, vinegar, sugar, salt, dillweed, onion powder and garlic powder.

2. Bring mixture to a boil; cover, reduce heat, and simmer 15 minutes.

3. Add beans, carrots, and celery.

4. Return mixture to a boil; cover, reduce heat, and simmer 5 minutes, until crisp tender.

5. Place vegetables in a shallow container; pour vinegar mixture over vegetables.

6. Cover and chill at least 8 hours.

7. Drain vegetables before serving.

CURRIED MUNCH MIX

[Makes 6 cups]

Here is a snack mix that is low in calories, but high in flavor. It's a great combination to take along when hiking.

1½ cups toasted oat cereal
1½ cups corn bran cereal
1   cup crisp wheat square cereal
1   cup crisp corn square cereal
1   cup miniature pretzels
½   cup raisins
2   tablespoons reduced calorie margarine, melted
1   teaspoon paprika
½   teaspoon curry powder
¼   teaspoon garlic powder

1. Combine oat cereal, corn bran cereal, wheat square cereal, corn square cereal, pretzels and raisins in large bowl or large resealable plastic bag.

2. Mix together melted margarine with paprika, curry and garlic powder.

3. Pour well mixed margarine mixture over cereal. Mix well or shake to evenly combine ingredients.

ASPARAGUS ROLLUPS

[Serves 12]

Here is a first class springtime appetizer. I like to have these completed rollups in the refrigerator waiting to be baked just before guests arrive.

12 **slices good quality white bread, crusts removed**
1   **[8 ounce] container whipped cream cheese**
2   **tablespoons chopped fresh or freeze dried chives**
8   **slices bacon, cooked and crumbled**
24 **fresh asparagus spears, partially cooked**
3   **tablespoons melted margarine or butter**
    Parmesan cheese

1. Use a rolling pin to flatten each slice of bread.

2. Combine cream cheese, chives, and bacon; stir well.

3. Spread bread with cheese mixture, covering to edges.

4. Place 2 asparagus spears on each slice of bread; roll up and place seam side down on greased or parchment lined cookie sheet. [Cover and refrigerater 4-6 hours, if desired]

5. Brush each rollup with melted margarine and sprinkle with Parmesan cheese.

6. Bake in preheated 400 degree oven for 10-12 minutes or until bread is lightly browned.

Honey-Glazed Chicken Wings

[Makes 10-12 appetizer servings]

Few guests will be able to resist these finger licking good meaty chicken bites. Equally popular with efficient cooks, this fantastic marinade is a quick way to give tiny wing pieces full bodied flavor.

3-4 pounds chicken wings
1   cup honey
½   cup soy sauce
2   tablespoons sesame or vegetable oil
2   tablespoons shredded fresh gingerroot
2   tablespoons sliced green onions
2   tablespoons ketchup
⅛   teaspoon garlic powder

1. Cut off and discard wingtips of chicken wings; cut wings in half at joint. Place wing pieces in a resealable plastic bag or 9x13-inch baking dish.

2. In 2 cup glass measurer, measure honey. Add soy sauce, oil, fresh gingerroot, green onions, ketchup and garlic powder. Stir to evenly combine.

3. Pour mixture over wing pieces, turning to coat evenly. Seal or cover and chill at least 1 hour.

4. Transfer wings to foil covered 10x15x1-inch jellyroll pan; bake, uncovered, in preheated 375 degree oven for 45 minutes, turning once.

5. Transfer to serving platter.

Savory Stuffed Mushrooms

[Makes 10-12 appetizer servings]

For lots of folks, hot stuffed mushrooms are near the top of the appealing appetizer list. This variation can easily be made ahead of time allowing the cook freedom to enjoy family and friends.

1   pound medium to large fresh mushrooms
¼   cup finely chopped onion
⅛   teaspoon garlic powder
¼   cup grated Parmesan cheese
¼   cup dry bread crumbs
½   teaspoon dried oregano leaves

[continued]

SAVORY STUFFED MUSHROOMS [continued]

¼ teaspoon salt
⅛ teaspoon pepper

1. Separate mushroom caps from stems; set caps aside.

2. Finely chop mushroom stems. [I like to use a food processor.]

3. In medium mixing bowl, combine chopped mushroom stems, onion, garlic powder, Parmesan cheese, bread crumbs, oregano leaves, salt and pepper. Mix lightly.

4. Press mixture firmly into mushroom caps, mounding on top.

5. Place stuffed mushrooms in ungreased 9x13-inch baking pan.

6. Cover and refrigerate up to 4 hours before baking, if desired.

7. Bake in preheated 350 degree oven 18-23 minutes or until thoroughly heated.

8. Serve immediately.

JAN'S APPETIZER CHEESE TARTS

[Makes 2 tarts, each serves 4]

My friend, Jan Mora, has a special flair for choosing interesting recipes. So I was not surprised when I tasted this wonderful way she served Brie cheese. Look for small rounds of this cheese near the Deli department of most grocery stores.

1 [4 ounce] can refrigerated crescent rolls
2 [4 and ¼ ounce] Brie cheese rounds,
1 egg, beaten
Sliced almonds or chopped pistachio nuts
Assorted fresh fruit, like apples and pears

1. Divide dough into two rectangles and place on parchment lined or greased cookie sheet. Shape rectangles in 8x5-inch pieces.

2. Place a Brie round in the middle of each rectangle. Bring up dough around cheese so it is completely enclosed. Place seam side down.

3. Brush with beaten egg and sprinkle with almonds or pistachios.

4. Bake in preheated 375 degree oven 12-15 minutes.

5. Let stand 2 or 3 minutes. Serve with crisp fresh wedges of apples and pears.

APPETIZER HAM BALLS

[Makes 10-12 appetizer servings]

As is true with most meatball recipes, these appetizer ham balls will be popular in any crowd. At serving time, keep these morsels hot in a chafing dish or electric fondue pot along with a good supply of decorative toothpicks.

1   egg
1   **pound ground cooked ham**
½   **pound lean ground pork**
1   **cup soft bread crumbs**
⅓   **cup milk**
2   **tablespoons chopped green onions**
½   **teaspoon prepared mustard**
1   **[12 ounce] jar chili sauce**
1   **[12 ounce] jar peach preserves**

1. In large mixing bowl, beat egg with a fork.

2. Add ham, pork, bread crumbs, milk, green onions and mustard; mix well.

3. Form into 1-inch balls.

4. Place in ungreased 10½ x 15½ inch jelly roll pan.

5. Bake in preheated 350 degree oven for 25-30 minutes or until light brown.

6. In large saucepan, combine chili sauce and preserves. Add ham balls, simmer 25-30 minutes, stirring occasionally.

Microwave

In step **4**, put half of the ham balls on microwave roasting rack. Microwave on 100% power 5-6 minutes or until meatballs are done, rotating rack once. Repeat procedure.

In step **6**, combine chili sauce and preserves in 3 quart microwave-safe casserole. Microwave on 100% power 5-6 minutes, until piping hot, stirring mixture twice. Add meatballs and microwave on 100% power 4-7 minutes, until hot, stirring once or twice.

CHICKEN SATAY APPETIZER

[Makes 24 appetizers]

My friend, Mary Kaye Merwin of Long Island, New York, likes interesting appetizer recipes like this chicken idea of Southeast Asia origin. Traditionally, Satay consists of bite-sized pieces of meat threaded on skewers and served with a spicy sauce.

2   whole chicken breasts, skinned, boned
    Salt and pepper, if desired
24 [6-inch] bamboo skewers
1   medium green bell pepper, cut into 1-inch squares
1   medium red bell pepper, cut into 1-inch squares
½   cup creamy peanut butter
½   cup vanilla lowfat yogurt
¼   cup water
2   tablespoons soy sauce
4   drops hot pepper sauce

1. Cut chicken into lengthwise strips about ½-inch wide.

2. If desired, lightly salt and pepper.

3. On each skewer, thread 1 piece each of green and red pepper and 1 strip chicken accordion style.

4. Place skewers on lightly greased 10½ x 15 ½ inch jelly roll pan.

5. In medium saucepan, combine peanut butter, yogurt, water, soy sauce and hot pepper sauce. Blend well.

6. Remove ¼ cup of the sauce; brush on chicken pieces.

7. Bake in preheated 375 degree oven for 12-15 minutes or until chicken is no longer pink.

8. Meanwhile, heat remaining sauce over low heat until hot, stirring occasionally.

9. Serve chicken and peppers with warm sauce.

Microwave

In step **5**, combine peanut butter, yogurt, water, soy sauce and hot pepper sauce in 1 quart microwave-safe casserole. Blend well.

In step **8**, microwave on 100% power 1-2 minutes, stirring every 30 seconds.

SKINNY POTATO SKINS

[Serves 8-10]

The clue to these great potato skins is the long 2 hour baking time. This gives the skin of the potato time to become crisp and draw away from the pulp. I'm fortunate that my husband, George, likes this recipe so much that he often helps by scooping out the pulp of the baked potatoes.

6   large baking potatoes
¼   cup skim milk
¼   cup liquid margarine type spread
¼   cup fat reduced cheddar cheese

1. Wash potatoes, leaving the outer skins moist.

2. Bake in preheated 350 degree oven 2 hours.

3. Remove from oven and cool until easy to handle.

4. Cut potato in half. Put cut surface on cutting board and divide in half again, forming four potato skins from each potato.

5. Take out some of the pulp; save for another use.

6. Mash remaining pulp close to skin with fork.

7. Drizzle each skin with ½ teaspoon milk.

8. Then squeeze ½ teaspoon liquid margarine spread on each potato skin.

9. Sprinkle each skin with ½ teaspoon cheddar cheese.

10. At this point, skins may be frozen for later use, if desired.

11. Broil potato skins for 2-4 minutes until cheese is melted.

Microwave

In step **11**, put 4-6 potato skins on microwave-safe plate. Microwave on 100% power 1-2 minutes, until cheese melts.

SEASONED SPINACH BALLS

[Makes 7-8 dozen]

This great make ahead appetizer recipe comes to me via my friend, Avalene Swanson of New Richmond, Wisconsin. Stored in the freezer, these flavorful spinach tidbits are ready to bake whenever needed.

6   **eggs**
¾   **cup margarine or butter, melted**
½   **cup grated Parmesan cheese**
1   **tablespoon garlic salt**
1   **teaspoon pepper**
1   **cup finely chopped onion**
1   **[8 ounce] package herb seasoned stuffing mix, finely crushed**
2   **[10 ounce] packages frozen chopped spinach, thawed, drained, and thoroughly squeezed dry**

1. In large mixing bowl, beat eggs with rotary beater or wire whisk.

2. Add melted margarine, Parmesan cheese, garlic salt and pepper. Beat or whisk to thoroughly combine ingredients.

3. Add onion, stuffing mix and spinach. Mix well.

4. Cover and chill for several hours.

5. Shape into 1-inch balls. Put balls on large tray. Freeze.

6. When spinach balls are frozen, package in airtight containers. Store in the freezer.

7. Just before serving, bake frozen spinach balls in preheated 350 degree oven for 15-20 minutes or until piping hot.

8. Serve immediately.

Microwave

In step **7**, microwave 6 spinach balls, covered with waxed paper on 100% power 3-4 minutes or until set, rotating ½ turn once during cooking.

SPARKLING APPLE CIDER

[Serves 6]

Sparkling fruit juices have recently grown in popularity. Although they are widely available, it's fun to create your own with concentrated frozen fruit juice and sparkling mineral water.

1 **[12 ounce] can frozen apple juice concentrate, thawed and undiluted**
1 **[23 or 25 ounce] bottle sparkling mineral water, chilled**

    1. In large pitcher, combine apple juice concentrate and mineral water, stirring gently.

    2. Serve immediately over crushed ice.

CHERRY BUBBLE

[Makes 20 half cup servings]

When a red sugar free punch is requested, here is the perfect recipe. The delightful color comes from the cherry gelatin and the flavor boost is derived from the fruit juices and carbonated beverage.

1 **cup boiling water**
1 **[0.3 ounce] package sugar-free cherry flavored gelatin**
1 **quart apple juice**
⅓ **cup lemon juice**
1 **liter sugar-free ginger ale, chilled**

    1. Combine boiling water and gelatin. Stir thoroughly until gelatin is dissolved.

    2. Add apple juice and lemon juice; chill.

    3. To serve, add ginger ale.

    4. Garnish with lots of ice.

PUNCH FOR A BUNCH

[Serves 50]

Several years ago, my friends at Battle Creek Chapel Hill United Methodist Church shared this delicious punch recipe with me. It's the punch they often use for wedding receptions, but would be appropriate whenever a large group gathers together.

1 [46 ounce] can pineapple juice, chilled
1 [46 ounce] can grapefruit juice, chilled
2 [46 ounce] cans red Hawaiian punch
1 [6 ounce] can frozen lemonade concentrate, thawed
1 [6 ounce] can frozen orange juice concentrate, thawed
2 cups cold water
1 [2 liter] bottle ginger ale, chilled

1. In very large punch bowl, combine pineapple juice, grapefruit juice, Hawaiian punch, lemonade concentrate, orange juice concentrate and 2 cups water. Stir gently.

2. Just before serving, add ginger ale.

3. Garnish with ice ring or lots of ice cubes.

APRICOT REFRESHER

[Makes 22 half cup servings]

It doesn't take long to put this refreshing apricot based beverage together. Family members and friends are certain to applaud your creative effort.

1 [46 ounce] can apricot nectar, chilled
1 [12 ounce] can frozen lemonade concentrate, thawed
1 liter lemon-lime carbonated beverage, chilled

1. In punch bowl or large non-metal pitcher, combine apricot nectar and lemonade concentrate; mix well.

2. Just before serving, add carbonated beverage.

GOLDEN BUBBLE

[Makes 24 half cup servings]

Popular punch recipes have refreshing flavor, yet use everyday ingredients and are easy to combine. I think this bubbly beverage is an excellent example of that criteria.

1   **quart apple juice, chilled**
1   **quart orange juice, chilled**
1   **[6 oz.] can frozen lemonade concentrate, thawed [¾ cup]**
1   **liter lemon-lime carbonated beverage or ginger ale, chilled**

1. In punch bowl or other large container, combine apple juice, orange juice and lemonade concentrate.

2. Add carbonated beverage and stir gently.

3. Add lots of ice as garnish.

STRAWBERRY PUNCH

[Makes 28 half cup servings]

Strawberry flavored gelatin gives this thirst quenching punch its natural color and appealing flavor base. To freeze strawberries for garnish, just wash and gently pat dry fresh strawberries with stems left on for added color. Arrange berries in single layer on cookie sheet; freeze until firm.

1   **[3 ounce] package strawberry flavored gelatin**
1   **cup boiling water**
1   **[12 ounce] can frozen pink lemonade concentrate, thawed**
1   **[6 ounce] can frozen orange juice concentrate, thawed**
6   **cups cold water**
1   **liter ginger ale, chilled**
   Frozen whole strawberries for garnish, if desired.

1. Dissolve gelatin in boiling water; cool to lukewarm.

2. In large punch bowl, combine gelatin mixture, lemonade concentrate, orange juice concentrate and cold water.

3. Just before serving, gently stir in ginger ale.

4. Add frozen strawberries and ice for garnish, if desired.

RASPBERRY COOLER

[Serves 12]

Even though this bright red punch reminds me of holidays like Christmas, Valentines or the Fourth of July, it can be served any time of year. This fruity blend is worthy of consideration the next time the menu calls for a beverage.

1   [12 ounce] can frozen raspberry juice blend, thawed
1   [6 ounce] can frozen lemonade, thawed [¾ cup]
2   cups cold water
2   liters ginger ale, chilled

1. In punch bowl or large pitcher, combine raspberry juice, lemonade and water. Stir to combine.

2. Gently add ginger ale.

3. Garnish with lots of ice.

APPLE GRAPE DELIGHT

[Makes 28 half cup servings]

Here in southwest Michigan, apple and grape flavors are often teamed together when it's autumn harvest time. However, this punch knows no season, it's delicious any time of year.

1½ quarts [6 cups] apple juice, chilled
1   quart [4 cups] grape juice, chilled
1   [6 ounce] can frozen lemonade concentrate, thawed
1   liter lemon-lime carbonated beverage, chilled

1. In large punch bowl, combine apple juice, grape juice and lemonade concentrate.

2. Just before serving, add carbonated beverage, stirring gently.

3. Add lots of ice for garnish .

CRANBERRY SPARKLE

[Serves 8]

Even though cranberry juice cocktail is delicious by itself, there are festive occasions when a sparkling punch is desired. This blend of fruit juices is a delicious way to meet that need.

1 quart [4 cups] cranberry juice cocktail, chilled
1 cup grapefruit juice, chilled
1 cup orange juice, chilled
½ cup sugar
2 cups ginger ale, chilled

1. In large non-metal pitcher or punch bowl, combine cranberry juice cocktail, grapefruit juice, orange juice and sugar. Stir to dissolve sugar.

2. Just before serving, add ginger ale, stirring gently.

3. Add ice so punch stays icy cold.

FRUIT COOLER

[Makes 30 half cup servings]

I've always liked fruit punch recipes that called for ingredients that could be kept on hand until needed. That way it's just a matter of opening cans and bottles when serving time arrives. This fruit based recipe is an excellent example.

1 [46 ounce] can pineapple juice, chilled
1 [12 ounce] can frozen orange juice concentrate, thawed
1 [12 ounce] can frozen lemonade concentrate, thawed
1 [12 ounce] can frozen limeade concentrate, thawed
2 cups cold water
1 liter ginger ale, chilled
   Fresh fruit slices for garnish, if desired

1. In punch bowl, combine pineapple juice, orange juice concentrate, lemonade concentrate, limeade concentrate and water. Mix well.

2. Just before serving, add ginger ale, stirring gently.

3. Add ice and fresh fruit slices for garnish, if desired.

OLD-FASHIONED PINK LEMONADE

[Serves 6]

What fun it is to serve this tart and tangy pink lemonade on a hot summer day. Only you know that the pretty color comes from cranberry juice cocktail.

4½ cups water, divided
1 cup sugar
1 cup lemon juice
½ cup cranberry juice cocktail, chilled

1. In medium saucepan, combine 2 cups water and sugar.

2. Heat and stir just until sugar dissolves. Cool.

3. In large non-metal pitcher, combine sugar syrup, remaining 2 and ½ cups water, lemon juice, and cranberry juice cocktail.

4. Serve in pretty glasses over ice cubes.

Microwave

In step **1**, combine 2 cups water and sugar in 1 quart microwave-safe measurer.

In step **2**, microwave on 100% power for 2-3 minutes, stirring once until sugar dissolves.

SUGAR FREE "GOOP"

[Makes 50 half cup servings]

If you need sugar free-punch for a crowd, here is an updated version of a favorite punch, called "Goop", that is found in my first cookbook, House Specialties. Because fruit flavored soft drink mix comes in lots of colors and flavors, it's easy to color coordinate the punch with the occasion.

2 [0.31 ounce] envelopes sugar free soft drink mix [your choice of color and flavor]
2 quarts water, chilled
1 [46 ounce] can unsweetened pineapple juice, chilled
1 liter sugar-free ginger ale, chilled

1. In large punch bowl or other non-metal container, combine soft drink mix, water, and pineapple juice. Mix well.

2. Just before serving, add ginger ale.

3. Add lots of ice and enjoy.

STRAWBERRY TEA

[Makes 25 half cup servings]

This lovely hot beverage is a thoughtful way to welcome guests as they gather for brunch, dinner or just to chat. Traditionally, tea has enhanced fruit juices and this recipe is no exception.

2   **cups boiling water**
4   **regular size tea bags**
6   **[3-inch] sticks cinnamon, broken into pieces**
1   **teaspoon whole cloves**
1   **[46 ounce] can pineapple juice**
1   **[6 ounce] can frozen orange juice concentrate, thawed**
1   **[6 ounce] can frozen lemonade concentrate, thawed**
1   **[3 ounce] package strawberry-flavored gelatin**
2   **cups water**

1. Pour 2 cups boiling water over tea bags; cover. Let stand 12-15 minutes. Remove tea bags.

2. Combine cinnamon and cloves in a cheese cloth bag.

3. In Dutch oven, combine tea, spice bag, pineapple juice, undiluted orange juice concentrate, undiluted lemonade concentrate, strawberry gelatin, and 2 cups water.

4. Bring to a boil.

5. Cover, reduce heat, and simmer 45 minutes.

6. Remove and discard spices.

7. Serve hot.

Microwave

In step **3**, use microwave-safe punch bowl.

In steps **4** and **5**, microwave on 100% power 45-60 minutes, stirring occasionally.

Hot Spiced Cider

[Serves 10-12]

Steaming mugs of hot apple cider warm both the body and the spirit on a crisp autumn day. This nicely spiced sugar-free version will be popular with family members and friends.

1   **medium orange, sliced**
2   **quarts unsweetened apple cider**
1   **teaspoon whole allspice**
16 **whole cloves**
2   **[2-inch] sticks cinnamon**

    1. Combine sliced orange, apple cider, whole allspice, cloves and cinnamon in large saucepan.

    2. Bring to a boil; reduce heat and simmer 15 minutes.

    3. Strain mixture. Serve piping hot.

Hot Cran Apricot Steamer

[Serves 6]

It doesn't take long to combine equal parts of cranberry juice cocktail, apricot nectar and pineapple juice. Meld the flavors together with gentle heat and a lovely hot beverage emerges for your tasting pleasure.

2   **cups cranberry juice cocktail**
2   **cups apricot nectar**
2   **cups pineapple juice**

    1. In large saucepan, combine cranberry juice cocktail, apricot nectar and pineapple juice

    2. Simmer over low heat 10 to 15 minutes until hot.

    3. Serve in attractive mugs or cups.

Microwave

    In step **1**, combine cranberry juice cocktail, apricot nectar and pineapple juice in 2 quart microwave-safe measurer.

    In step **2**, micwave on 100% power 8-10 minutes until hot.

HOT LEMONADE TEA

[Serves 6-8]

For years the flavors of lemon and tea have teamed together in pleasing fashion. This steaming hot variation is great for sipping, relaxing and curling up with a good book.

6   **cups water**
¼   **cup sugar**
1   **[6 ounce] can frozen lemonade concentrate, [¾ cup]**
3   **cinnamon sticks**
4   **tea bags**
     Clove studded lemon wedges for garnish, if desired

1. In large saucepan, combine water, sugar, lemonade concentrate and cinnamon sticks.

2. Bring to a boil; remove from heat.

3. Add tea bags; cover.

4. Let stand 5 minutes.

5. Remove tea bags. Strain, if desired.

6. Pour into cups. Garnish with clove studded lemon wedges, if desired.

Microwave

In step **1**, combine water, sugar, lemonade concentrate and cinnamon sticks in 2 quart microwave-safe measurer.

In step **2**, microwave on 100% power 10-12 minutes, or until mixture boils.

Entrees

For years, I've had the philosophy that to provide cooks with a selection of exciting entrees truly captures the essence of recipe sharing. Once the main attraction of any menu is planned, the other components come easily.

These significant entrees have been chosen because of their outstanding flavor, ease of preparation and variety of protein sources.

From chili made with turkey and black beans to a quick skillet method of cooking a pound of fresh shrimp, these ideas are designed to make menu planning easy.

Contents

TURKEY BLACK-BEAN CHILI

[Serves 6-8]

Our family has settled on this recipe as their favorite way to enjoy brimming bowls of heart healthy chili. Black beans seem to add class to the recipe, but kidney beans can be used....just change the name of the recipe.

Vegetable spray
1   **pound ground raw turkey**
½   **cup chopped onion**
2   **[28 ounce] cans whole tomatoes with juice, crushed**
2   **[15 or 16 ounce] cans black beans, rinsed and drained**
1   **[4 ounce] can diced green chilies, mild, medium or hot**
1   **tablespoon instant beef bouillon or beef base**
¼   **teaspoon garlic powder**
3   **teaspoons chili powder**
1   **teaspoon ground cumin**

1. Spray Dutch oven with vegetable spray.

2. Brown crumbled turkey and onion in Dutch oven until meat is cooked. Drain.

3. Add tomatoes, beans, chilies, beef bouillon or base, garlic powder, chili powder and cumin. Stir well.

4. Heat to boiling, stirring often. Reduce heat to low and simmer, stirring occasionally, 30 minutes.

Microwave

In step **1**, spray hard plastic colander with vegetable spray.

In step **2**, crumble turkey and onion in colander. Rest colander in microwave-safe pie plate or dish. Microwave on 100% power 3 minutes. Break up meat with a fork or small hand chopper. Microwave on 100% power 2-3 more minutes until meat is cooked. Chop with fork. Drain.

WILD RICE CHEESY POTATO SOUP

[Serves 8-10]

This soup is one way our family enjoys the treasured wild rice my Aunt Jessie and Uncle Bill Howell of Minneapolis, Minnesota send us each Christmas. It's a great comfort food during those winter days that greet each new year.

½   cup wild rice, uncooked
2   cups water
4   slices bacon, cut into pieces
¼   cup chopped onion
2   [10¾ ounce] cans cream of potato soup, undiluted
3   cups milk
2½ cups grated sharp Cheddar cheese

1. In medium saucepan, combine wild rice and water. Cook over low heat 45 minutes or until rice is tender. Drain.

2. In Dutch oven, fry bacon pieces and onion until bacon is crisp, stirring frequently.

3. Drain cooked bacon and onion thoroughly on paper towel.

4. Return drained bacon and onion to Dutch oven.

5. Add cooked wild rice, cream of potato soup, milk, and cheese.

6. Gently heat over low heat, stirring frequently until hot and all cheese is melted.

7. Serve and enjoy.

Microwave

In step **2**, combine bacon pieces and onion in 3 quart microwave-safe soup tureen or casserole. Microwave on 100% power 4-6 minutes, stirring two or three times, until bacon is crisp.

In step **6**, microwave on 100% power 15-18 minutes, stirring every 5 minutes.

LIGHT CLAM CHOWDER

[Serves 4]

This classic soup is slimmed down by using skim milk and less bacon, without losing in-depth flavor. That's good news for those of us who are always on the lookout for lighter versions of popular recipes.

1   **slice bacon**
1   **cup diced peeled potatoes**
¼   **cup chopped onion**
2   **[6½ ounce] cans minced clams, drained, reserving liquid**
¼   **cup flour**
½   **teaspoon salt**
⅛   **teaspoon pepper**
3   **cups skim milk**
¼   **cup shredded carrot**

1. Cook bacon in large saucepan until crisp. Remove bacon; set aside.

2. Stir potatoes, onion and reserved clam liquid into bacon drippings; bring to a boil. Reduce heat; cover and simmer 10 minutes.

3. In 1-quart jar with tight-fitting lid, combine flour, salt, pepper and milk; shake until smooth.

4. Gradually stir flour mixture into vegetables. Add carrots.

5. Cook over medium heat 10 minutes or until thickened and vegetables are crisp-tender, stirring frequently.

6. Stir in clams. Heat gently, stirring frequently. DO NOT BOIL.

7. Garnish each serving with bacon that has been crumbled.

Microwave

In step **1**, put bacon in 3 quart microwave-safe soup tureen or casserole. Microwave on 100% power 1 to 2 minutes or until bacon is crisp. Remove bacon; set aside.

In step **2**, stir in potatoes, onion and carrots; cover with lid or vented plastic wrap. Microwave on 100% power 3 to 4 minutes or until vegetables are crisp-tender, stirring once.

In step **4**, add flour, salt and pepper to vegetables; blend well. Stir in clam liquid and milk.

[continued]

LIGHT CLAM CHOWDER [continued]

In step **5**, microwave on 100% power for 10-12 minutes, or until mixture comes to a boil, stirring twice during cooking.

In step **6**, add clams. Microwave on 100% power 1 to 2 minutes or until thoroughly heated.

GOLDEN OYSTER STEW

[Serves 4]

Even though I don't usually put cheese in oyster stew, I have found it to be a wonderful addition. Maybe that's because my Wisconsin dairyland "roots" are so deep.

½   **cup chopped onion**
½   **cup chopped celery**
2   **tablespoons margarine or butter, melted**
2   **cups [8 ounces] sliced fresh mushrooms**
2   **tablespoons flour**
2   **cups milk**
1   **cup shredded sharp Cheddar cheese [4 ounces]**
1   **[10 and ½ ounce] can cream of potato soup, undiluted**
1   **[2-ounce] jar diced pimiento, undrained**
¼   **teaspoon salt**
⅛   **teaspoon pepper**
⅛   **teaspoon hot pepper sauce**
1   **[12 ounce] container oysters, undrained**

1. Saute onion and celery in margarine until tender. Add mushrooms and cook about 2 minutes.

2. Add flour and cook 1 minute, stirring constantly.

3. Gradually add milk; cook over medium heat, stirring frequently until mixture is thickened and bubbly.

4. Stir in cheese, soup, pimiento, salt, pepper, and hot pepper sauce.

5. Cook over medium heat, stirring often, until cheese melts and mixture is thoroughly heated.

6. Add oysters and oyster liquid; reduce heat and simmer 5 to 8 minutes or until edges of oysters curl.

TURKEY MINESTRONE

[Serves 10]

Here is a tried and true heart smart soup recipe. Lowfat ground turkey teams up with an interesting variety of garden vegetables in true Italian style.

1	**pound ground raw turkey**
½	**cup chopped onion**
5	**cups water**
2	**tablespoons beef bouillon granules or beef base**
2	**cups shredded cabbage**
1	**cup diced carrots**
1	**cup diced zucchini**
1	**[14 and ½ to 16 ounce] can whole tomatoes, crushed**
¼	**teaspoon garlic powder**
1	**teaspoon basil leaves**
1	**[10 ounce] package frozen cut green beans**
¼	**cup snipped fresh parsley**
	Salt and pepper to taste, if desired

1. Spray bottom of Dutch oven with vegetable spray. Crumble ground turkey into Dutch oven. Add onion.

2. Cook over medium heat until turkey is cooked and onion is tender. Drain.

3. Stir in water, beef bouillon, cabbage, carrots, zucchini, tomatoes, garlic powder, and basil.

4. Bring mixture to a boil. Reduce heat and simmer 15-20 minutes until vegetables are tender.

5. Stir in beans and parsley. Simmer until beans are cooked.

Microwave

In step **1**, spray hard plastic colander with vegetable spray. Crumble ground turkey into colander. Add onion. Rest colander in microwave-safe pie plate or dish.

In step **2**, microwave on 100% power 5-7 minutes or until turkey is no longer pink, stirring once to break turkey into pieces. Drain.

In step **3**, put cooked turkey in microwave-safe soup tureen or large casserole. Stir in water, beef bouillon, cabbage, carrots, zucchini, tomatoes, garlic powder and basil.

[continued]

TURKEY MINESTRONE [continued]

In step **4**, microwave on 100% power 20-30 minutes, stirring several times.

In step **5**, microwave on 100% power 5-10 more minutes or until thoroughly heated.

SALMON CORN CHOWDER

[Serves 8]

It doesn't take long to make this thick and creamy chowder. Just chop onion and celery; then quickly open four cans. In a matter of minutes you're serving hot steaming bowls of homemade soup. Yes, you really did make it yourself...

1   [15 and ½ ounce] can salmon
2   tablespoons margarine or butter
¾   cup chopped onion
¾   cup chopped celery
1   [10 and ¾ ounce] can cream of potato soup
1   [10 and ¾ ounce] can cream of celery soup
2   cups milk
1   [15-17 ounce] can cream style corn
¼   teaspoon dried thyme leaves, crushed

1. Flake salmon; do not drain. Set aside.

2. In Dutch oven, melt margarine. Saute onion and celery in margarine until tender.

3. Stir in salmon, potato soup, celery soup, milk, cream style corn and thyme leaves.

4. Heat over medium heat, stirring occasionally.

5. Serve.

Microwave

In step **2**, omit margarine. Put onion, celery and 1 tablespoon water in microwave-safe soup tureen or 3 quart casserole. Microwave on 100% power 2-3 minutes until vegetables are tender, stirring once.

In step **4**, microwave on 100% power 8-10 minutes until piping hot, stirring two or three times.

CRAB CAULIFLOWER BISQUE

[Serves 4-6]

Busy cooks will welcome the convenience of a package of frozen cauliflower in cheese sauce when they decide to make this classy crab bisque. Just add crusty bread sticks and fresh fruit to complete a quick and easy menu.

2	tablespoons margarine or butter
¼	cup chopped onion
¼	cup chopped celery
2	tablespoons flour
1	teaspoon instant chicken bouillon
¼	teaspoon white pepper
2	cups milk
1	[10 ounce] package cauliflower frozen in cheese sauce
1	[6 or 8 ounce] package frozen imitation crab, thawed & chopped
	Chopped fresh parsley for garnish, if desired

1. In medium saucepan, melt margarine. Saute onion and celery in melted margarine.

2. Blend in flour, chicken bouillon and pepper; cook until smooth and bubbly.

3. Gradually stir in milk; cook until mixture is hot, stirring constantly.

4. Add cauliflower. Reduce heat; cover and simmer 15-18 minutes or until cauliflower is tender, stirring often.

5. Break up any large pieces of cauliflower with fork or small chopper.

6. Add crab. Heat gently, stirring frequently.

7. Pour into individual soup bowls.

8. Garnish with chopped fresh parsley.

Microwave

In step **1**, put margarine in 2 quart microwave-safe soup tureen or casserole. Microwave on 100% power 30 seconds or until melted. Stir in onions and celery; microwave on 100% power 1-2 minutes, stirring once.

In step **2** and step **3**, stir in flour, chicken bouillon, pepper and milk. Blend well. Heat on 100% power 4-8 minutes until hot, stirring every 2 minutes.

[continued]

CRAB CAULIFLOWER BISQUE [continued]

In step **4**, add cauliflower. Microwave on 100% power 6-8 minutes, stirring every 2 minutes, until cauliflower is tender.

In step **6**, add crab. Microwave on 80% power 4-6 minutes, stirring several times, until hot.

SPLIT PEA CHICKEN CHOWDER

[Serves 8]

Split peas team up with chicken in this wholesome nutrition packed chowder. It is helpful for the busy cook to note that because split peas require no overnight soaking, all ingredients efficiently go into the soup pot at the same time.

8   **cups water**
2   **tablespoons plus 2 teaspoons instant chicken bouillon**
    or 8 chicken bouillon cubes
1   **[16 ounce] package green split peas, rinsed & drained**
1   **cup finely chopped onions**
1½ **cups finely chopped carrots**
¾   **cup finely chopped celery**
2   **medium potatoes, peeled & diced**
3   **cups diced cooked chicken**
⅛   **teaspoon thyme leaves**
⅛   **teaspoon pepper**
¼   **teaspoon salt, if desired**

1. In 5 or 6 quart Dutch oven, combine water, bouillon, split peas, onions, carrots, celery, potatoes, chicken, thyme and pepper.

2. Bring mixture to a boil. Reduce heat; cover.

3. Simmer 45-60 minutes or until chowder has thickened and split peas are thoroughly cooked, stirring occasionally.

4. Season with salt, if desired.

ASPARAGUS QUICHE

[Serves 6-8]

It was a red letter day when I opened the mail and found this delicious recipe from my friend, Mary Lindell, of Darlington, Wisconsin. Within 24 hours, I created and tasted this delicate quiche and realized there was a mouth watering reason she'd shared the recipe with me.

4   **eggs**
1½ **cups milk**
½   **teaspoon salt**
¼   **cup finely chopped onions**
½   **cup finely chopped celery**
½   **cup finely chopped fresh asparagus**
1   **cup diced ham**
2   **tablespoons flour**
1   **cup [4 ounces] shredded Swiss or Cheddar cheese**
     Ground nutmeg, if desired
1   **10-inch unbaked pastry shell**

1. In large mixing bowl, gently beat together eggs, milk and salt.

2. Add onions, celery, asparagus and ham.

3. Toss cheese with flour.

4. Gently stir cheese into egg mixture.

5. Pour into unbaked pastry shell.

6. Sprinkle with nutmeg, if desired

7. Bake in preheated 325 degree oven 45-50 minutes or until silver knife inserted in the center of the quiche comes out clean.

Hash-Brown Quiche

[Serves 6-8]

Cooks that shy away from pastry in quiche recipes will find this hash-brown crust idea the perfect substitution. Filled with ham and cheese, it's guaranteed to please palates of all ages.

3   cups refrigerated hash-brown potatoes
    or
3   cups loose-pack frozen hash-brown potatoes, thawed
3   tablespoons margarine or butter, melted
1   cup diced or shredded cooked ham
1   cup [4 ounces] shredded sharp Cheddar cheese
1   cup [4 ounces] shredded Monterey Jack cheese
4   drops hot pepper sauce
2   eggs
½   cup milk
¼   teaspoon seasoned salt

1. If you are using frozen hash-brown potatoes, press hash browns between paper towels to remove moisture.

2. Press hash browns onto bottom and up sides of a 9-inch pie plate to form a crust.

3. Drizzle melted margarine over crust.

4. Bake crust in preheated 425 degree oven 20-25 minutes, until lightly browned. Remove from oven.

5. Reduce oven temperature to 350 degrees.

6. Toss together the ham, Cheddar cheese, Monterey Jack cheese and hot pepper sauce. Place in crust.

7. Beat the eggs, milk and seasoned salt together to form a smooth mixture. Pour over ham and cheese.

8. Bake, uncovered, in the 350 degree oven 25-30 minutes or until knife inserted near the center comes out clean.

9. Let stand for 10 minutes before serving, if time permits.

MEXICAN EGG BAKE

[Serves 6-8]

Family members will hop out of bed on the first wake up call when this "south of the border" entree is on the breakfast menu. It's a great way to start the day.

6   **corn tortillas**
12   **eggs**
½   **cup milk**
1   **cup [4 ounces] shredded sharp Cheddar cheese**
1   **cup [4 ounces] shredded Monterey jack cheese**
¼   **cup chopped red or green bell pepper**
1   **[4 ounce] can diced green chilies, mild, medium or hot**
    Salsa or picante sauce, heated if desired

1. Warm tortillas as directed on package; arrange in bottom of well-greased 8x12-inch baking dish overlapping edges of tortillas as needed.

2. In mixing bowl, beat eggs and milk until well blended.

3. Stir in cheese, pepper and chilies.

4. Pour egg mixture over tortillas.

5. Bake in preheated 350 degree oven 25-35 minutes or until knife inserted in center comes out clean.

6. Serve with salsa or picante sauce, heated if desired.

STUFFED FRENCH TOAST

[Serves 6-9]

Our Minnesota niece, Kelly House, thinks this is the greatest way in the whole world to enjoy French Toast. We agree, it is simply scrumptious. The toast can be fried ahead of time, covered, and refrigerated. Just before serving arrange pieces on a lightly buttered baking sheet and bake uncovered in a preheated 350 degree oven for 10-15 minutes or until thoroughly heated.

1   [8 ounce] package cream cheese, softened
1   teaspoon vanilla
½   cup coarsely chopped pecans
1   [16 ounce] loaf French bread
4   eggs
½   pint whipping cream [1 cup]
½   teaspoon nutmeg
½   teaspoon vanilla
1-2 tablespoons butter or margarine
1   [12 ounce] jar apricot preserves
½   cup orange juice

1. In small mixing bowl, beat together cream cheese and 1 teaspoon vanilla until fluffy. Stir in pecans. Set aside.

2. Slice bread into 18 [1¼-inch] slices.

3. Cut a pocket into top of each slice.

4. Fill with 1 tablespoon cream cheese mixture. Gently squeeze pocket opening together.

5. In flat bowl, beat eggs, whipping cream, nutmeg and ½ teaspoon vanilla.

6. Using tongs, quickly dip filled bread slices into egg mixture, stirring mixture to distribute nutmeg.

7. Cook on lightly buttered griddle over medium-low heat until both sides are golden.

8. In small saucepan, heat preserves and orange juice until hot; serve over stuffed toast.

Microwave

In step 8, combine preserves and orange juice in 1 quart microwave-safe measurer. Microwave on 100% power 1-3 minutes, until hot, stirring once or twice.

PRALINE BRUNCH TOAST

[Serves 6-8]

My friend, Norma Ostrander from Bay City, Michigan, often serves this scrumptious variation of French Toast to family and friends. To me, it's make ahead feature is reason enough to remember this idea for a special family breakfast or overnight guests.

8   **eggs or egg substitute**
1½ **cups half and half coffee cream**
1   **tablespoon brown sugar**
2   **teaspoons vanilla**
8   **[¾ inch thick] slices French bread**
½   **cup margarine or butter**
¾   **cup brown sugar**
½   **cup maple syrup**
¾   **cup coarsely chopped pecans**

1. In mixing bowl, beat together eggs, half and half, 1 tablespoon brown sugar and vanilla.

2. Pour half of the egg mixture into a 9x13-inch baking pan.

3. Place bread slices in mixture.

4. Pour remaining egg mixture over top of bread.

5. Cover and refrigerate several hours or overnight.

6. Melt margarine in another 9x13 inch baking pan.

7. Stir in ¾ cup brown sugar and maple syrup.

8. Sprinkle with pecans.

9. Place soaked bread slices on nuts.

10. Pour any remaining egg mixture over bread.

11. Bake in preheated 350 degree oven until puffed and lightly browned, about 30-35 minutes.

12. To serve, invert onto plates and sprinkle with any nuts that remain in baking dish.

SAVORY SAUSAGE STRATA

[Serves 8]

Stratas have traditionally been a favorite make ahead breakfast or brunch entree. In this variation, ground sausage shows itself off in style. Just add a thoughtful assortment of fresh fruit along with steaming mugs of coffee for a memorable morning meal.

1½ **pounds bulk ground sausage**
6 **slices good quality white bread**
1 **cup shredded mozzarella cheese**
4 **eggs**
2 **cups milk**
½ **teaspoon salt**
½ **teaspoon dry mustard**

1. In a large skillet, cook sausage until brown, frequently breaking up pieces. Drain well.

2. Cut bread into cubes.

3. In an 8x12-inch baking dish, evenly spread half of the sausage.

4. Top the sausage with bread cubes, then shredded mozzarella cheese. Sprinkle with remaining sausage.

5. In a mixing bowl, beat together eggs, milk, salt and mustard until evenly combined. Pour over sausage mixture.

6. Cover and refrigerate for 3 to 24 hours.

7. Bake, covered, in a preheated 325 degree oven for 30 minutes.

8. Uncover; bake for 15-20 minutes more or till a knife inserted near the center comes out clean.

9. Let stand for 10 minutes before serving.

Microwave

In step 1, spray a hard plastic colander with vegetable spray. Rest colander in microwave-safe pie plate. Crumble sausage into colander. Microwave on 100% power 8-9 minutes, breaking meat apart twice during cooking time.

HAPPY HEART STRATA

[Serves 6]

This type of make ahead breakfast casserole has long been a friend to the cook with weekend or holiday guests. Here is a scrumptious healthy heart version that's lower in fat and cholesterol and features skim milk, low-fat cheese and egg substitute.

Vegetable cooking spray
3   **cups cubed French bread**
¾   **cup diced lean cooked ham**
2   **tablespoons diced sweet red pepper**
1   **cup shredded, reduced-fat sharp Cheddar cheese [4 ounces]**
1⅓ **cups skim milk**
¾   **cup egg substitute**
¼   **teaspoon dry mustard**
¼   **teaspoon onion powder**
⅛   **teaspoon white pepper**

1. Spray an 8-inch square baking dish with vegetable cooking spray.

2. Place bread cubes in baking dish.

3. Layer ham, red pepper and cheese over bread; set aside.

4. Combine milk, egg substitute, dry mustard, onion powder and white pepper. Thoroughly mix together; pour over layered ingredients.

5. Cover and refrigerate 8-24 hours.

6. Remove from refrigerator; let stand 30 minutes.

7. Bake, uncovered, in preheated 350 degree oven 30 minutes, until mixture is set.

8. Serve immediately.

VEGETABLE LASAGNA

[Serves 8]

If you've been on the search for a light vegetable lasagna, look no further. Here is a grand plan that is so delicious, it gives the traditional higher fat lasagna healthy competition.

[continued]

VEGETABLE LASAGNA [continued]

6   **uncooked lasagna noodles**
½   **cup chopped onion**
1   **cup thinly sliced fresh mushrooms, [2½ ounces]**
⅜   **teaspoon garlic powder**
2   **tablespoons water**
1   **cup lowfat part-skim ricotta or cottage cheese**
½   **cup shredded carrot**
1   **[10 ounce] package frozen chopped spinach, thawed, squeezed dry**
2   **egg whites**
¼   **cup grated Parmesan cheese, divided**
½   **teaspoon salt**
1   **[14 ounce] jar spaghetti sauce**
1   **cup shredded lowfat part-skim mozzarella cheese**

1. Cook lasagna noodles to desired doneness as directed on package. Drain; rinse with hot water.

2. Spray medium nonstick skillet with nonstick cooking spray. Add onion, mushrooms and garlic powder; cook and stir 1 minute.

3. Add water; cover and cook 3-4 minutes until crisp-tender.

4. In small bowl, combine ricotta cheese, carrots, spinach and egg whites, 2 tablespoons Parmesan cheese and salt; mix well.

5. In ungreased 8x12 inch baking dish, layer half of the cooked noodles, half of the sauce, half of the mushroom mixture and half the ricotta cheese mixture; repeat layers.

6. Sprinkle with mozzarella cheese and remaining 2 tablespoons Parmesan cheese.

7. Bake in preheated 350 degree oven 30-35 minutes until hot and bubbly. Let stand 10 minutes before serving.

Microwave

In step **2**, put onion, mushrooms and garlic powder in 1 quart microwave-safe bowl. Cover with vented plastic wrap. Microwave on 100% power 2-3 minutes until crisp-tender.

In step **3**, omit water.

In step **7**, cover with vented plastic wrap. Microwave on 100% power 5 minutes. Rotate dish ½ turn. Continue to microwave on 50% power for 15-20 minutes until thoroughly heated in center.

GROUND BEEF OLE

[Serves 8-10]

When the gang gathers together for fun and feasting, this south of the border flavored casserole will disappear in double quick time. Sprinkle the baked mixture with assorted toppings or supply an ample selection so each person can make their own personal Ground Beef Ole.

1	**pound ground beef**
½	**cup chopped onion**
2	**cups water**
1	**[8 ounce] can tomato sauce**
1	**tablespoon chili powder**
⅛	**teaspoon garlic powder**
¼	**teaspoon dried oregano, crushed**
1	**[15 ounce] can red kidney beans, drained**
8	**ounces tortilla chips, coarsely crushed**

Toppings like: Shredded lettuce, shredded cheddar or Monterey Jack cheese, chopped tomatoes, sliced green onion, sliced black or green olives, and sour cream

1. In skillet, brown ground beef and onion. Drain fat.

2. Return beef to skillet. Add water, tomato sauce, chili powder, garlic powder and oregano. Mix well.

3. Pour half of the mixture into a 9x13 inch baking dish.

4. Top with half of the beans and half the chips.

5. Repeat layering.

6. Cover and bake in preheated 350 degree oven for 30 minutes or until thoroughly heated.

7. Serve with assortment of toppings.

Microwave

In step **1**, spray hard plastic colander with vegetable cooking spray. Crumble ground beef and onion in colander. Set colander in microwave-safe dish. Microwave on 100% power 3 minutes; break up meat with chopper or fork. Microwave an additional 3-4 minutes on 100% power, until meat is no longer pink.

In step **2**, combine drained beef, water, tomato sauce, chili powder, garlic powder and oregano in large mixing bowl. Mix well.

CHEESEBURGER BAKE

[Serves 8]

You'll smack your lips in disbelief when you taste this family pleasing recipe. How can just four ingredients evolve into such a winner? When hungry kids and grandchildren ask, "What's for supper?" pop this casserole in the oven.

2   **pounds lean ground beef**
1   **[10 and ¾ ounce] can condensed golden mushroom soup**
1   **[11 ounce] can condensed cheddar-cheese soup**
1   **[20 ounce] package frozen, fried crinkle-cut potatoes**
      Toppings like ketchup, mustard, pickles and onion

1. In a large skillet, cook the ground beef until brown.Thoroughly drain off fat.

2. Place cooked meat in the bottom of a 9x13 inch baking dish.

3. In mixing bowl, combine condensed golden mushroom soup and the condensed cheddar cheese soup.

4. Spread soup mixture over the meat in the casserole.

5. Sprinkle the frozen crinkle-cut potatoes over the top of the casserole.

6. Bake in a preheated 350 degree oven 50-60 minutes or until potatoes are golden.

7. Garnish and/or serve with toppings of your choice.

Microwave

In step **1**, spray a hard plastic colander with vegetable spray. Crumble half of the ground beef in colander. Microwave on 100% power 5-7 minutes, breaking up meat halfway through cooking time. Drain. Repeat procedure.

TACO/BEEF/NOODLE BAKE

[Serves 8]

This hearty casserole is certain to receive high marks from family members who enjoy south of the border flavors. It's also the type of recipe that can be frozen before baking, if you desire.

1   **pound ground beef**
½   **cup chopped onion**
1   **[15 ounce] can tomato sauce**
½   **cup water**
1   **[1¼ ounce] package taco seasoning mix**
9-10 ounces medium egg noodles
2   **teaspoons instant beef bouillon or beef base**
2   **cups [1 pound] small curd cottage cheese**
¼   **cup light or regular sour cream**
1   **tablespoon flour**
¼   **cup sliced green onion**
1   **cup [4 ounces] shredded mozzarella cheese**

1. In large skillet, brown ground beef and onion, stirring often to crumble meat. Drain well.

2. Add tomato sauce, water and taco seasoning mix; bring to a boil. Reduce heat and simmer 10 minutes.

3. Cook noodles according to package directions; drain.

4. Combine noodles, beef bouillon or base, cottage cheese, sour cream, flour and green onion.

5. Spoon noodle mixture into a greased 2 and ½ quart casserole. Top with meat mixture.

6. If desired, cover and refrigerate up to 24 hours or cover tightly and freeze for later use.

7. Bake uncovered in preheated 350 degree oven 25-35 minutes, until hot and bubbly. [Longer if frozen.]

8. Sprinkle with mozzarella cheese and bake an additional 5 minutes or until cheese melts.

[continued]

Taco/Beef/Noodle Bake [continued]

Microwave

> In step **1**, spray hard plastic colander with vegetable spray. Crumble ground beef and onion in colander. Rest colander in microwave-safe pie plate or dish. Microwave on 100% power 5-7 minutes until brown, breaking up meat once during cooking. Drain.

> In step **2**, microwave mixture in 2 quart microwave-safe casserole on 100% power 5-8 minutes, stirring two or three times.

Speedy Soy Marinade

[Makes 1½ cups]

I have always been partial to recipes that use common everyday ingredients. That must be the reason this marinade idea is one of my favorites. It's the perfect answer when you're in the mood for grilled or broiled beef, pork or chicken and need just a splash of seasoning.

½	**cup vegetable oil**
½	**cup soy sauce**
½	**cup lemon juice**
3	**tablespoons ketchup**
½	**teaspoon garlic powder**
¼	**teaspoon ground pepper**

> **1.** In 2 cup glass measurer, combine oil, soy sauce, lemon juice, ketchup, garlic powder and pepper. Whisk to evenly combine ingredients.

> **2.** Put marinade in resealable plastic bag or in shallow dish. Add beef, pork or chicken.

> **3.** Close or cover; marinate in refrigerator 4 hours or overnight, turning occasionally.

> **4.** Remove meat from marinade.

SWEDISH MEATBALLS

[Serves 6-8]

Most families give meatballs high ratings. I'm certain this Swedish variation will be a winner too. The traditional cream based sauce adds real class to tender meatballs.

1	egg
¼	cup milk
1	pound ground beef
½	pound ground pork
¾	cup dry bread crumbs
¼	cup chopped onion
1	teaspoon salt
¼	teaspoon ground nutmeg
⅛	teaspoon pepper
3	tablespoons melted margarine or pan drippings
3	tablespoons flour
¾	cup water
1	cup half and half coffee cream
1½	teaspoons beef bouillon granules or beef base
	Snipped fresh parsley

1. In large mixing bowl, beat together egg and milk.

2. Add ground beef, ground pork, bread crumbs, onion, salt, nutmeg, and pepper.

3. Shape mixture into 1-inch balls. There should be about 48 meatballs.[For easy shaping, dip hands into cold water from time to time.]

4. Place meatballs on ungreased 10x15 inch jelly roll pan. Bake uncovered in preheated 350 degree oven until light brown, about 20 minutes.

5. Remove meatballs to serving dish; keep warm.

6. Place margarine or drippings in saucepan; stir in flour.

7. Cook over low heat, stirring constantly, until mixture is smooth and bubbly. Remove from heat.

8. Stir in water, half and half and bouillon. Heat to boiling, stirring constantly. Boil and stir 1 minute.

9. Pour sauce over meatballs; heat if necessary.

10. Sprinkle with chopped fresh parsley.

[continued]

SWEDISH MEATBALLS [continued]

Microwave

In step **3**, place about 2 dozen meatballs in 8x12 inch microwave safe dish. Cover with waxed paper.

In step **4**, microwave on 100% power 4-7 minutes, or until meatballs are cooked and firm, rotating dish once, if desired.

In step **6**, use microwave-safe 2 quart measurer.

In step **7**, microwave on 100% power 30 seconds.

In step **8**, microwave on 100% power 4-7 minutes, stirring every minute or two until thick.

In step **9**, microwave on 80% power 8-12 minutes.

TACO BISCUIT PIE

[Serves 4-6]

When my friend, Nan Banks of Chetek, Wisconsin, gets home after a busy day of teaching school, this taco flavored pie is a great quick entree. Just add fresh fruit to complete a very fast menu.

1   **[10 ounce] can refrigerated biscuits**
1   **pound lean ground beef or ground turkey**
1   **[15 or 16 ounce] can kidney beans, undrained**
1   **[1.25 ounce] package taco seasoning mix**
1   **cup shredded sharp Cheddar cheese [4 ounces]**
½   **cup crushed corn chips**
½   **cup shredded lettuce**
1   **medium tomato, chopped**

1. Separate dough into 10 biscuits. Arrange 3 biscuits on bottom of ungreased 9-inch pie plate and 7 biscuits around sides; press biscuits to form crust. [Biscuits will form scalloped edge around rim of pan].

2. In large skillet, brown ground beef; drain.

3. Stir in beans and seasoning mix. Reduce heat; simmer 5 minutes.

4. Spoon hot meat mixture into biscuit-lined pan.

5. Bake in preheated 400 degree oven 12-16 minutes or until crust is golden brown.

6. Immediately top with cheese and corn chips.

7. Sprinkle with lettuce and tomato.

8. Allow to cool 5 minutes before cutting into wedges.

MYSTERY MINI MEAT LOAVES

[Serves 10-12]

When we tasted these delicious meat loaves at the home of Carol and Dick Bailey, we immediately wanted to identify the "mystery" ingredient. To our surprise, it was sauerkraut that had piqued our interest. However, the recipe is no secret since Carol willingly shared it with me.

½   **cup water**
½   **teaspoon instant beef bouillon**
1½ **cups soft bread crumbs**
3   **eggs, beaten**
1   **envelope dry onion soup mix**
3   **pounds lean ground beef**
1   **[12 ounce] bottle chili sauce**
1   **[16 ounce] can sauerkraut, drained and snipped**
1   **[16 ounce] can whole cranberry sauce**
1⅓ **cups water**
½   **cup brown sugar**

1. In large mixing bowl, mix together water and beef bouillon. Add soft bread crumbs and soak until water is absorbed.

2. Add beaten eggs and onion soup mix. Stir thoroughly.

3. Add ground beef. Mix with spoon and continue mixing with clean hands.

4. Shape into 10 or 12 individual loaves in lightly greased 9x13 inch baking pan.

5. Meanwhile, in medium saucepan, combine chili sauce, sauerkraut, cranberry sauce, water and brown sugar. Bring to a boil. Simmer over low heat for about 5 minutes.

6. Pour part of the sauce over meat loaves.

7. Bake in preheated 350 degree oven 60-70 minutes or until meat loaves are baked, basting with sauce as desired.

8. Heat remaining sauce and serve with meat loaves.

Microwave

In step **5**, use 2 quart microwave-safe measurer. Combine chili sauce, sauerkraut, cranberry sauce, water and brown sugar. Microwave on 100% power 10-15 minutes, stirring two or three times.

MIDWEST BEEF POT ROAST

[Serves 6-8]

Most of us who grew up here in the Midwest have fond memories of meals that originated with a less tender beef pot roast. We also remember how efficient cooks usually added potatoes and carrots part way through the cooking time for wholesome country flavor. Give this nostalgic recipe a try.

1   [3 to 4 pound] boneless beef chuck roast
1   cup chopped onion
1   cup sliced celery
1   [10 and ¾ ounce] can condensed tomato soup
1   tablespoon vinegar
2   teaspoons instant beef bouillon
1   teaspoon basil leaves, crushed
¼   teaspoon garlic powder
6   medium potatoes, peeled and quartered
6   carrots, peeled and cut into strips

1. Trim excess fat from meat.

2. Place meat in 3 quart casserole or slow cooker.

3. Add celery and onion.

4. In medium bowl, combine tomato soup, vinegar, beef bouillon, basil, and garlic powder. Mix well.

5. Pour tomato mixture over meat.

6. Cover. Bake in preheated 325 degree oven 2½ to 3 hours.

7. Approximately 1 hour before meat is cooked, add potatoes and carrots. Recover; continue baking.

Slow Cooker

In step **2**, put meat in slow cooker.

In step **6**, cover and cook in slow cooker and cook on low for 9-10 hours.

In step **7**, approximately 2 hours before meat is cooked add potatoes and carrots. Recover; continue cooking.

POPOVER PIZZA CASSEROLE

[Serves 8-10]

When the family gathers together for fun and fellowship, this is the recipe to remember. Grandparents to preschoolers love pizza and this casserole boasts lots of good Italian flavor.

1½ **pounds ground beef**
1 **[15 ounce] can tomato sauce**
1 **cup chopped onion**
1 **cup chopped green pepper**
½ **cup water**
1 **[1½ ounce] package spaghetti sauce mix**
1 **teaspoon dried oregano leaves, crushed**
⅛ **teaspoon garlic powder**
 Several dashes hot pepper sauce
¼ **cup margarine or butter, melted**
1 **cup milk**
1 **tablespoon vegetable oil**
2 **eggs**
1 **cup flour**
2 **cups [8 ounces] shredded mozzarella cheese**
½ **cup [2 ounces] grated Parmesan**

1. In a 12 inch skillet, cook the ground beef till brown. Drain well.

2. To drained, cooked ground beef in skillet, add tomato sauce, onion, green pepper, water, spaghetti sauce mix, oregano, garlic powder and hot pepper sauce. Bring to boiling. Reduce heat and simmer the mixture, covered, for 10 minutes.

3. Meanwhile, in a small bowl, beat together melted margarine, milk, oil and eggs for 1 minute on medium speed of an electric mixer. Add the flour and beat for 2 more minutes.

4. Put meat mixture into a 9x13-inch baking pan; sprinkle with mozzarella. Top with flour mixture.

5. Sprinkle with Parmesan.

6. Bake in preheated 400 degree oven for about 30 minutes or until puffed and golden.

7. Let casserole stand for 10 minutes before eating.

[continued]

POPOVER PIZZA CASSEROLE [continued]

Microwave

> In step **1**, spray hard plastic colander with vegetable spray. Set colander in microwave-safe pie plate. Crumble ground beef in colander. Microwave on 100 % power 7-9 minutes, breaking up meat twice during cooking. Drain well.

> In step **2**, put drained cooked ground beef, tomato sauce, onion, green pepper, water, spaghetti sauce mix, oregeno, garlic powder and hot pepper sauce in 2 quart microwave-safe measurer. Microwave on 100% power 8-10 minutes, stirring once or twice.

BROILED LAMB CHOPS FOR TWO

[Serves 2]

When the occasion calls for a special dinner for two, lamb chops are the perfect entree suggestion. Broiled to perfection in just minutes, there is plenty of time to enjoy each other.

4   **[1-inch thick] lamb chops**

1. Trim excess fat from lamb chops, if necessary.

2. Place chops on rack in broiler pan.

3. Place broiler pan so chops are 3-4 inches from heat.

4. Broil until brown, approximately 6 minutes.

5. Turn chops using tongs; broil until brown, approximately another 6 minutes.

6. Season with salt and pepper, if desired.

7. Serve immediately.

GYROS ROAST

[Serves 8-10]

We are so glad that our nephew, Chris House, from Minnesota, shared this dynamite grill recipe with us. He reports, and we agree, it is really easier than it sounds.

1   **[3-4 pound] leg of lamb, boned**
2½ **pounds boneless beef round steak**
¼   **cup dried oregano leaves**
2   **teaspoons dried dill weed**
2   **teaspoons garlic powder**
½   **teaspoon ground thyme**
1½ **teaspoons salt**
1   **teaspoon ground pepper**
     Olive oil

1. Pound lamb and beef steak on both sides with meat mallet until each piece of meat measures about 12x14 inches.

2. Combine oregano, dill, garlic powder, thyme, salt and pepper, crushing with back of spoon until fine textured, but not powdered.

3. Place lamb on cutting board; brush top lightly with oil and sprinkle with ⅓ of the herb mixture.

4. Pound herbs into surface of lamb with meat mallet.

5. Lay round steak on top of lamb; brush top lightly with oil and sprinkle with ½ the remaining herb mixture.

6. Pound herbs into surface of beef with meat mallet. Roll up meats as tightly as possible, starting at short end.

7. Tie securely in several places with string.

8. Brush outside with oil; rub with remaining herb mixture.

9. Insert meat thermometer so that tip is in the center of the roast.

10. Place roast in center of grill and cook in covered grill over medium heat until internal temperature registers 140 degrees, about 1½ hours.

11. Turn roast every 45 minutes; outside of meat will become very dark and crusty.

12. Remove meat and let stand 10 to 15 minutes.

13. Slice thinly and serve with pocket bread, sliced tomatoes, sliced onions, shredded lettuce and sauce of your choice.

BERRY BARBECUED PORK ROAST

[Serves 8-12]

Cranberries are a wonderful accompaniment for pork as well as poultry. In this clever recipe, these pungent berries team with barbecue flavors to enhance a popular pork loin roast.

4   **cups fresh or frozen cranberries**
1   **cup sugar**
½   **cup commercial barbecue sauce**
½   **cup orange juice**
1   **[4-6 pound] pork loin roast**

1. Combine cranberries, sugar, barbecue sauce and orange juice in a large saucepan, mixing well.

2. Bring to a boil over medium heat, stirring constantly. Continue boiling without stirring, 5 minutes; set aside.

3. Place roast, fat side up, on rack in shallow pan.

4. Insert meat thermometer in center of roast.

5. Roast, uncovered, in preheated 325 degree oven allowing 30-35 minutes per pound.

6. When pork is done, thermometer will register 170 degrees.

7. During the last 30 minutes of roasting time, baste meat frequently with cranberry barbecue sauce.

8. Let roast stand 10-15 minutes before carving.

9. Serve with remaining sauce.

Microwave

In step **1**, combine cranberries, sugar, barbecue sauce and orange juice in 3 quart microwave-safe casserole.

In step **2**, cover casserole with lid or vented plastic wrap. Microwave on 100% power 8-12 minutes, stirring twice, until berries are cooked. [Longer time is needed if cranberries are frozen]

Dijon Pork Chops

[Serves 4]

Dijon mustard has a smooth, tart, yet pleasing flavor and is considered by many connoisseurs to be one of the finest mustards available at the supermarket. No wonder it's the perfect mustard to compliment these delicious baked pork chops.

4   **[¾-inch thick] lean boneless pork chops**
½   **cup dry bread crumbs**
3   **tablespoons Dijon mustard**
3   **tablespoons lemon juice**

1. Trim all visible fat from pork chops.

2. Place crumbs on piece of waxed paper or in shallow dish.

3. In another shallow dish, combine mustard and lemon juice; blend well.

4. Spray a 9x13-inch baking pan with vegetable cooking spray.

5. Dip both sides of each pork chop in mustard mixture, then in bread crumbs to coat.

6. Place coated chops in spray-coated pan.

7. Bake in preheated 375 degree oven for 30-40 minutes until pork is no longer pink, turning once half way through baking.

STIR-FRY PORK

[Serves 2]

Lightning quick to fix, this stir-fry plan for pork may soon become one of your standby menu ideas. I like to keep Frozen Fruit Cups found on page 139 in the freezer to serve with this popular entree.

1	**cup water**
2	**tablespoons soy sauce**
1	**tablespoon plus 1 teaspoon cornstarch**
1	**teaspoon sugar**
¼	**teaspoon ginger**
¼	**teaspoon garlic powder**
⅛	**teaspoon salt**
⅛	**teaspoon pepper**
1	**tablespoon vegetable oil**
8	**ounces thinly sliced boneless pork, cut in ½-inch strips**
2	**cups frozen vegetable combination like broccoli, cauliflower and carrots, thawed**
2	**slices onion, separated into rings**
1	**cup fresh bean sprouts**
	Chow mein noodles or hot cooked rice

1. In small bowl, combine water, soy sauce, cornstarch, sugar, ginger, garlic powder, salt and pepper. Mix well. Set aside.

2. Heat oil in medium nonstick skillet over medium-high heat.

3. Add pork; stir fry 2-3 minutes or until pork is no longer pink.

4. Add thawed frozen vegetables and onion; stir-fry for 2-3 minutes or until vegetables are crisp-tender.

5. Stir sauce into vegetables; cook until thickened and bubbly, stirring constantly.

6. Add bean sprouts; heat thoroughly.

7. Serve over chow mein noodles or hot cooked rice.

BROCCOLI-HAM AU GRATIN

[Serves 8]

Broccoli and ham have been great flavor companions for years. Here they are star attractions in a make-ahead and easy-to-carry casserole. It's the perfect idea for your next potluck meal.

½   cup onion, chopped
1   tablespoon margarine or butter, melted
1   [11 ounce] can Cheddar cheese soup, undiluted
1   [8 ounce] package sliced sharp cheddar cheese, cubed
½   teaspoon garlic powder
1   [8 ounce] can sliced mushrooms, drained
1   [10 ounce] package frozen chopped broccoli, thawed & drained
3   cups unsalted cooked rice
3   cups diced cooked ham
1   [2 ounce] jar diced pimiento, drained
1   [2.8 ounce] can fried onions

1. Saute onion in margarine in a Dutch oven.

2. Add soup, cheese, and garlic powder; heat and stir until cheese melts.

3. Add mushrooms, broccoli, rice and ham. Mix well. Stir in pimiento.

4. Spoon mixture into a greased 8x12 inch baking dish.

5. Cover and chill up to 24 hours, if desired.

6. To bake, remove from refrigerator, and let stand at room temperature 30 minutes.

7. Bake, covered, in preheated 350 degree oven for about 40 minutes or until hot and bubbly.

8. Uncover. Sprinkle with onions and bake 5-10 minutes more.

Microwave

In step 1, saute onion in margarine in 3 quart microwave-safe casserole on 100% power 2-3 minutes, stirring once.

In step 2, add soup, cheese and garlic powder. Microwave on 100% power 3-5 minutes, stirring every minute.

In step 7, microwave on 80% power probing to 160 degrees.

In step 8, microwave on 80% power 3-4 minutes.

SAUSAGE AND RICE SKILLET

[Serves 6-8]

One dish meals have long been a favorite menu idea with busy cooks and active family members. This wholesome example is cleverly seasoned with chili powder and cumin.

1   **pound link smoked sausage, thinly sliced**
½   **cup chopped onion**
½   **cup chopped green pepper**
1½ **cups converted long grain rice**
2   **cups water**
1   **[14½ ounce] can stewed tomatoes, undrained**
⅔   **cup picante sauce or salsa, mild, medium or hot**
1   **teaspoon salt**
½   **teaspoon chili powder**
½   **teaspoon ground cumin**

1. Cook sausage in 12-inch skillet over medium heat until it starts to sizzle.

2. Add onion and green pepper; cook, stirring occasionally, until tender.

3. Add rice; mix well.

4. Stir in water, tomatoes, picante sauce, salt, chili powder and cumin.

5. Bring to boil; reduce heat.

6. Cover and simmer 20 minutes or until liquid is absorbed.

7. Garnish with green pepper strips or rings, if desired.

8. Sprinkle generously with grated Parmesan cheese.

HEARTY PORK 'N BEAN BAKE

[Serves 10-12]

This blue ribbon variation of baked beans is chuck full of meaty lean pork cubes. A wonderful in-depth flavor is developed by long, slow cooking. Add potato salad, fresh fruit and crusty French bread slices for a great casual menu.

½   **cup chopped onion**
1   **[48 ounce] jar cooked Great Northern beans**
1½ **cups brown sugar**
1½ **cups ketchup**
3   **tablespoons prepared mustard**
½   **teaspoon salt**
1½ **pounds lean 1-inch pork cubes**

1. In large mixing bowl, combine onion, beans, brown sugar, ketchup, mustard and salt. Mix thoroughly.

2. Gently stir in pork cubes.

3. Place mixture in 2 ½ or 3 quart beanpot or casserole.

4. Bake in preheated 300 degree oven, uncovered, for 5-6 hours or until beans are thickened.

5. These beans may be cooked in a slow cooker on the low setting for 8-10 hours.

GOLDEN CHICKEN ROLLS

[Serves 12]

Here is a wonderful entree that will wait patiently in the refrigerator until baking time. It takes all the rush out of pre-meal preparation, allowing the cook time to enjoy family and friends who have gathered together.

12   **boneless chicken breast halves, skinned**
12   **thin slices boiled or baked ham**
12   **thin slices Swiss cheese**
½   **cup margarine or butter, melted**
2½ **cups soft bread crumbs**
¼   **cup grated Parmesan cheese**

1. Flatten chicken, using flat side of a meat mallet.

2. Place 1 slice of ham and 1 slice of Swiss cheese on each.

3. Roll up like a jellyroll, folding in sides to hold ham and cheese. Secure with uncolored round toothpick.

4. On piece of waxed paper, combine bread crumbs and Parmesan cheese.

5. Dip each roll in melted margarine and then in bread crumb mixture.

6. Place rolls on lightly greased 10 ½ x 15 ½-inch jelly roll pan.

7. Cover and refrigerate up to 24 hours.

8. Remove cover. Bake in preheated 350 degree oven 40-50 minutes or until golden.

CRANBERRY CHICKEN

[Serves 6]

The contrasting flavors of cranberries and poultry family members have been teamed together for years. So it is no surprise that chicken marinated and baked in a cranberry based sauce is a first class entree. Use cut up chicken pieces for family meals or boneless chicken breasts for company fare. Last, but not least, note the make ahead feature of this dynamite recipe.

1   [16 ounce] can whole cranberry sauce
1   [8 ounce] bottle reduced calorie Russian salad dressing with honey
    or regular Russian dressing [1 cup]
1   envelope regular dry onion soup mix
3   pounds meaty chicken pieces

1. In a bowl, combine cranberry sauce, salad dressing and soup mix. Mix well. Set aside.
2. Rinse chicken; pat dry with paper towels. Remove and discard skin.
3. Arrange pieces in one layer in a 9x13-inch baking dish.
4. Pour cranberry mixture over chicken pieces.
5. Cover and chill the chicken mixture in the refrigerator for several hours or overnight.
6. Bake the chicken mixture, uncovered, in preheated 300 degree oven about 1½ hours or until chicken is done, stirring glaze and spooning it over chicken once or twice.

CHICKEN BROCCOLI LASAGNA

[Serves 8-12]

Whenever lasagna is mentioned, smiles of approval can be seen on the faces of hungry guests and family members. However, you may get a surprised look or two when they learn that this lasagna shows off chicken and broccoli. After one taste of this recipe, those smiling faces will reappear.

9   uncooked lasagna noodles
¼   cup margarine or butter
3   cups [8 ounces] fresh mushrooms, sliced
¼   teaspoon garlic powder
1   teaspoon lemon juice

[continued]

CHICKEN BROCCOLI LASAGNA [continued]

¼ cup flour
1 tablespoon chicken bouillon or chicken base
3 cups milk
2 cups cubed, cooked chicken
1 [10 ounce] package chopped broccoli, cooked and drained
1 [15 ounce] carton ricotta cheese
1 egg
2 tablespoons chopped fresh or freeze dried chives
2 cups [8 ounces] shredded mozzarella cheese
½ cup grated Parmesan cheese
2 tablespoons chopped fresh parsley

1. Cook lasagna noodles to desired doneness as directed on package. Drain; rinse with hot water.

2. In large saucepan, melt margarine; add mushrooms, garlic powder and lemon juice. Saute until mushrooms are tender, about 5 minutes.

3. Stir in flour and chicken bouillon or base; blend well. Add milk.

4. Cook over medium high heat until mixture thickens and boils, stirring constantly.

5. Stir in chicken and broccoli.

6. In medium bowl, combine ricotta cheese, egg and chives.

7. To assemble, spread about 1 cup sauce in ungreased 9x13 inch baking dish.

8. Layer ⅓ noodles, ⅓ ricotta mixture, ⅓ of the mozzarella, ⅓ of the sauce and ⅓ of the Parmesan cheese; repeat layers, ending with Parmesan on top.

9. Sprinkle with parsley.

10. Bake, uncovered, in preheated 325 degree oven for 45 minutes or until bubbly.

11. Let stand 10-15 minutes before serving.

Microwave

In step **2**, melt margarine in 2-3 quart microwave-safe casserole on 100% power 30 seconds. Add mushrooms, garlic powder and lemon juice. Microwave on 100% power 3-5 minutes until mushrooms are tender, stirring once or twice.

In step **4**, microwave on 100% power 6-8 minutes, until mixture thickens, stirring three or four times.

STIR-FRY CHICKEN AND BROCCOLI

[Serves 4]

Health conscious cooks are partial to the stir-fry method of cooking. They realize that it's a lowfat way to prepare nutrition rich vegetables as well as lean meats. In this recipe, broccoli and chicken are the featured "good for you" ingredients.

1 **egg white**
2 **boneless chicken breasts, skinned & cut into small pieces**
2 **tablespoons cornstarch, divided**
1 **cup water**
1½ **teaspoons instant chicken bouillon**
¼ **teaspoon ground ginger**
1 **tablespoon low sodium soy sauce**
   Cooking spray
1 **tablespoon vegetable oil**
⅛ **teaspoon garlic powder**
⅓ **cup sliced green onions**
3 **cups broccoli flowerets**
½ **large red pepper, sliced into strips**
4 **ounces sliced fresh mushrooms**

1. Gently beat egg white with rotary beater. Add chicken breast pieces and 1 tablespoon cornstarch. Let stand 15 minutes, if time permits.

2. Mix water with chicken bouillon, 1 tablespoon cornstarch, ginger and soy sauce. Reserve.

3. Heat wok or large skillet until hot.

4. Spray with cooking spray. Add chicken mixture; stir-fry until meat is no longer pink. Remove chicken from skillet.

5. Add 1 tablespoon oil, garlic powder and green onions. Stir-fry a few minutes.

6. Add broccoli and pepper strips; stir-fry 2-3 minutes.

7. Add mushrooms and stir-fry a minute.

8. Stir in water and chicken bouillon mixture. Heat to boiling, stirring constantly; boil and stir until sauce is thickened and clear.

9. Stir in chicken; cook until thoroughly heated.

10. Serve with rice, if desired.

CRISPY OVEN FRIED CHICKEN

[Serves 4]

Over the years chicken has lost its "skin" and many folks think deep fat frying of chicken is taboo. However, most of us still like chicken that is crispy. So, here is the answer. Fat-free egg white serves as an excellent binder for the crispy coating on these mouth-watering chicken pieces.

1½ **cups cornflakes cereal, crushed to ⅔ cup**
1 **teaspoon paprika**
½ **teaspoon garlic powder**
½ **teaspoon oregano leaves**
⅛ **teaspoon pepper**
1 **egg white**
2-3 **pounds meaty chicken pieces, skinned**

1. In food processor bowl with metal blade, crush cornflakes or put cornflakes into plastic bag and crush until fine.

2. Add paprika, garlic powder, oregano leaves and pepper. Pulse food processor to blend or shake well in plastic bag.

3. Put crumb mixture in plastic bag if mixture has been crushed in food processor bowl.

4. Place egg white in shallow bowl; beat slightly.

5. Dip chicken pieces in egg white.

6. Shake dipped chicken, 1 or 2 pieces at a time, in cereal mixture to coat.

7. Place on foil lined jelly roll pan.

8. Bake in preheated 400 degree oven about 45 minutes or until fork tender and juices run clear.

SARA'S SLOW COOKER CHICKEN AND RICE

[Serves 4-6]

Our daughter, Sara, learned to appreciate the slow cooker type of cooking appliance when she moved to an apartment, during her college years. She has always liked chicken and rice, so it's not surprising that this recipe has become a standby when there is no time to fix dinner.

2   cups water
2   teaspoons instant chicken bouillon
1   [6 ounce] package long grain and wild rice
4-6 meaty chicken pieces, skinned
     Salt and pepper
     Paprika

1. In slow cooker casserole, combine water, chicken bouillon and the rice with seasoning packet. Mix well.

2. Lightly sprinkle chicken pieces with salt, pepper and paprika.

3. Place chicken pieces over rice.

4. Cover slow cooker and cook on low 5 to 6 hours.

TURKEY TETRAZZINI

[Serves 8]

Tetrazzini recipes traditionally consist of turkey or chicken, pasta and a rich cream sauce. What a versatile way to combine familiar ingredients in a classy casserole type dish.

1   [7- 9 ounce package] uncooked spaghetti
¼   cup margarine or butter
8   ounces fresh mushrooms, sliced
3   tablespoons flour
2   teaspoons instant chicken bouillon
2   cups water
¾   cup half and half coffee cream
1   tablespoon chopped fresh parsley
⅛   teaspoon nutmeg

[continued]

TURKEY TETRAZZINI [continued]

Dash pepper
3 **cups cubed cooked turkey or chicken**
¾ **cup grated Parmesan cheese**
   Chopped fresh parsley for garnish

1. Cook spaghetti to desired doneness as directed on package. Drain; rinse and save for use in recipe.

2. Melt margarine in Dutch oven or large saucepan over medium heat.

3. Add mushrooms; cook until tender.

4. Stir in flour; cook 1 minute or until smooth and bubbly, stirring constantly.

5. Add chicken bouillon and water. Cook over medium heat until slightly thickened and bubbly, stirring constantly. Remove from heat.

6. Stir in half and half, 1 tablespoon parsley, nutmeg and pepper.

7. Add turkey and cooked spaghetti; toss with sauce.

8. Pour mixture into lightly greased 3 quart baking dish; sprinkle with Parmesan cheese.

9. Bake in preheated 350 degree oven for 30-35 minutes or until thoroughly heated.

10. Garnish with fresh parsley before serving.

Microwave

In step **2**, microwave margarine in 2 quart microwave-safe measurer on 100% power 30 seconds.

In step **3**, microwave mushrooms on 100% power 2-4 minutes, stirring several times.

In step **5**, microwave on 100% power 4-6 minutes, stirring every minute or two.

TURKEY CRANBERRY SAUTE

[Serves 4]

No longer do we need to wait for Thanksgiving to team turkey with cranberries. That's because, in most supermarkets you'll find an ample selection of fresh turkey cuts, and cranberries can be kept in the home freezer. Just follow these directions for a wonderful entree that takes less than half an hour to prepare.

1¼ **pounds fresh turkey breast tenderloins or slices**
Vegetable cooking spray
½ **cup chopped onion**
⅛ **teaspoon garlic powder**
1 **medium cooking apple, pared, cored and chopped**
½ **teaspoon sage leaves, crushed**
½ **teaspoon thyme leaves, crushed**
½ **cup fresh or frozen cranberries**
½ **cup unsweetened apple juice**
⅓ **cup chicken broth**
2 **tablespoons sugar**
Dash of ground nutmeg
Snipped parsley for garnish

1. Cut turkey in serving size pieces.
2. Spray nonstick skillet with vegetable cooking spray and heat over medium heat.
3. Saute turkey until light brown; remove from skillet.
4. In the same skillet, cook onion with garlic powder until tender, stirring frequently.
5. Stir in apple, sage and thyme. Cook 1 minute.
6. Add cranberries, apple juice, chicken broth, sugar and nutmeg. Stir.
7. Return turkey to skillet.
8. Heat to boiling; reduce heat.
9. Cover and simmer until turkey is tender and no longer pink, 20-25 minutes.
10. Serve turkey topped with sauce mixture.
11. Garnish with snipped parsley.

TURKEY BURGERS

[Serves 4 or 5]

I find that ground turkey needs a little "help" before it becomes a tasty turkey patty. Here is a recipe plan that has come to the rescue. Try them soon and judge for yourself.

1	**pound ground turkey**
1	**cup grated zucchini**
1	**cup fresh bread crumbs**
½	**cup finely chopped onion**
½	**teaspoon salt**
½	**teaspoon poultry seasoning**
	Freshly ground pepper to taste
1	**tablespoon vegetable oil**

1. In large mixing bowl, put turkey, zucchini, bread crumbs, onion, salt, poultry seasoning, and pepper.

2. Lightly toss together until well mixed.

3. Form the turkey mixture into 4 or 5 patties.

4. Heat the oil in a skillet over medium heat and cook the patties about 3-4 minutes on each side, or until done and the meat in the center has turned opaque and is no longer pink. If overcooked they will become dry.

Microwave

Freeze extra turkey burgers for reheating later in the microwave.

To reheat each frozen turkey burger, place on plate and cover with waxed paper. Microwave on Defrost [30% power] for 1-3 minutes. Microwave on 80% power for 2-4 minutes until hot.

SHRIMP AND ASPARAGUS A LA KING

[Serves 4]

This lovely creamed mixture is a perfect brunch or lunch suggestion. To add elegance to the menu, serve over patty shells. For a more casual event, try the quick and easy toast cups.

¼   cup margarine or butter
1   cup sliced fresh mushrooms
¼   cup flour
2   teaspoons instant chicken bouillon or base
2   cups milk
4   drops hot pepper sauce
6-8 ounces frozen cooked shrimp, thawed
2   cups fresh asparagus cuts, cook and drained
     or
1   [10 ounce] package frozen asparagus cuts, cooked & drained
4   patty shells or toast cups [see recipe below]

1. In saucepan, saute margarine and fresh mushrooms for a few minutes.

2. Stir in flour and chicken bouillon. Heat until bubbly.

3. Add milk and hot pepper sauce. Cook and stir over medium heat until thickened.

4. Stir in shrimp and asparagus. Heat until piping hot.

5. Serve over patty shells or toast cups.

Microwave

In step **1**, saute margarine and mushrooms in 2-quart microwave safe measurer on 100% power for 2-3 minutes, stirring once.

In step **2**, microwave on 100% power 30 seconds.

In step **3**, Microwave on 100% power 4-6 minutes, stirring two or three times until thickened.

In step **4**, microwave on 100% power 2-4 minutes.

TOAST CUPS:

Trim crusts from 4 slices of fresh bread; spread with soft margarine or butter. Press buttered side down into muffin cups. Bake in preheated 375 degree oven 10-15 minutes or until lightly toasted.

STUFFED FLOUNDER

[Serves 6]

Just when I was looking for an interesting fish recipe, my friend, Mary Koenig, shared this one with me. On days when I can't find flounder, I use orange roughy. Because the roughy fillets are too thick for a muffin cup, I put them in small bowls the size of a 10 ounce custard cup.

3 **large flounder fillets [about 1¼ pounds]**
  Pepper to taste
1 **tablespoon olive oil**
1½ **cups sliced mushrooms**
¼ **cup minced onion**
½ **cup diced carrots, cooked tender-crisp and drained**
1 **tablespoon minced fresh parsley**
½ **cup low calorie Italian salad dressing**

1. Cut fillets in half lengthwise. Sprinkle with pepper.

2. Roll up each fillet lengthwise and place in greased muffin cup or small dish.

3. In small skillet, heat olive oil. Saute mushrooms and onion in oil until soft. Do not brown.

4. Stir in carrots and parsley.

5. Stuff mixture into fish cavities.

6. Spoon dressing over fillets.

7. Bake in preheated 400 degree oven 15 minutes.

Microwave

In step **2**, roll up fillets and place in greased small microwave-safe dishes.

In step **3**, omit oil. Put mushrooms, onion, and uncooked carrots in 4 cup microwave-safe measurer. Add 1 tablespoon water. Cover with vented plastic wrap. Microwave on 100% power 2-3 minutes, until vegetables are tender, stirring once. Drain.

In step **7**, microwave three fillets at a time using the guideline of 4-6 minutes on 100% power.

Sweet and Sour Fish Kabobs

[Serves 4]

For years, I've enjoyed serving colorful kabobs to friends and family members. Here is a heart healthy plan, featuring fish, that has lots of eye appeal and is long on flavor.

½   cup ketchup
¼   cup sugar
3   tablespoons vinegar
2   tablespoons pineapple juice
2   tablespoons soy sauce
1   pound swordfish or other fish steaks, cut in squares
1   [8 ounce] can pineapple chunks, drained
1   red bell pepper, cut into squares
1   green bell pepper, cut into squares
1   [8 ounce] can water chestnuts, drained

1. Combine ketchup, sugar, vinegar, pineapple juice and soy sauce. Mix well.

2. Put fish in shallow dish or resealable bag. Pour marinade over fish and toss to evenly combine.

3. Cover or seal; refrigerate 30 minutes to 2 hours.

4. On metal skewers, alternate fish, pineapple, peppers and water chestnuts.

5. Place kabobs on oiled grill 4 to 6 inches from coals.

6. Brush with marinade; cook until fish flakes easily with fork, turning once and brushing frequently with marinade.

Shrimp Skillet

[Serves 2-4]

For fabulous fast flavor, this shrimp entree rates a gold star. Serve over rice or add a wholesome baked potato as a side dish for a menu that brings rave reviews.

2   teaspoons vegetable oil
1   pound shelled fresh or frozen medium-sized uncooked shrimp, thawed and deveined

[continued]

SHRIMP SKILLET [continued]

1   **medium onion, sliced**
1   **medium green pepper, sliced into thin strips**
⅜   **teaspoons garlic powder**
¼   **teaspoon salt**
1   **[14½ ounce] can stewed tomatoes, undrained**

> **1.** Heat oil in large skillet over medium-high heat.
>
> **2.** Cook shrimp, onion and green pepper until shrimp turns pink and vegetables are crisp-tender, stirring constantly.
>
> **3.** Add garlic powder, salt and tomatoes; cook and stir 2 to 3 minutes or until thoroughly heated.

TARRAGON GRILLED FISH

[Serves 4-6]

Fish fillets are pieces of fish that are cut lengthwise from the sides of the fish away from the backbone. In this recipe, tender fish fillets absorb the pungent flavor of tarragon by sprinkling dried herb leaves on both the fish and the hot coals.

1½-2 **pounds mild fish fillets, like orange roughy**
½   **teaspoon dried tarragon, crushed**
      White pepper to taste
2   **tablespoons dried tarragon, crushed**

> **1.** Lightly sprinkle fish fillets with ½ teaspoon tarragon leaves and pepper.
>
> **2.** Sprinkle 2 tablespoons tarragon over ash-covered hot coals.
>
> **3.** Oil fish basket or grill and put fish in place over coals to cook, about 5-10 minutes, until fish begins to flake when tested with fork.
>
> **4.** Turn once or twice.
>
> **5.** Watch carefully and enjoy.

OVEN FRIED FISH

[Serves 4]

Most quick and easy fish recipes, like this one, are designed to use many varieties of fish. Orange roughy, ocean perch, sole, or whitefish are excellent choices for this oven entree.

2	tablespoons margarine
¼	cup flour
¾	teaspoon onion salt
	Dash of pepper
2	egg whites or 1 egg, slightly beaten
1	tablespoon water
1	tablespoon lemon juice
1	pound favorite fish fillets
¾	cup crushed crackers or bread crumbs

1. Preheat oven to 350 degrees.

2. Melt margarine in 8x12 inch baking dish in oven.

3. On a piece of waxed paper or in a shallow bowl, combine flour, onion salt and pepper.

4. In medium bowl, combine egg whites or egg, water and lemon juice. Use a wire whisk to make certain ingredients are well blended.

5. Coat fish fillets with flour mixture; dip in egg mixture. Roll in crumbs.

6. Place fish in baking dish; turn to coat with melted margarine.

7. Bake in preheated 350 degree oven for 15-20 minutes or until fish flakes easily with fork.

Microwave

In step **2**, microwave margarine in microwave-safe 8x12-inch baking dish on 100% power for 30-45 seconds or until melted.

In step **3**, add ½ teaspoon paprika.

In step **7**, microwave on 100% power 5-6 minutes or until fish flakes easily with fork.

SEAFOOD RICE MEDLEY

[Serves 6-8]

Collections of creative casserole recipes are treasured by many cooks. This interesting seafood rice combination would easily be included in such a grouping. Ordinary ingredients are transformed into an entree with extraordinary flavor.

2   cups cooked rice
2   [4½ ounce] cans shrimp, drained & rinsed
6   ounces frozen imitation crab meat, thawed & shredded
1   [8 ounce] can sliced water chestnuts, drained
½   cup chopped onion
½   cup chopped celery
½   cup chopped green pepper
1   cup mayonnaise
1   cup tomato juice
⅛   teaspoon ground pepper
1   cup shredded sharp Cheddar cheese [4 ounces]
½   cup toasted slivered almonds

1. In mixing bowl, combine rice, shrimp, crab, water chestnuts, onion, celery, and green pepper. Toss lightly.

2. In small bowl, whisk together mayonnaise, tomato juice and pepper.

3. Add dressing to rice mixture. Stir gently.

4. Spoon mixture into greased 2-quart casserole.

5. Sprinkle cheese and almonds over top.

6. Bake in preheated 350 degree oven 35-45 minutes or until hot and bubbly.

DILLED SALMON ALASKAN STYLE

[Serves 4]

When our friends, Ardyce and Dave Curl, returned from one of their Alaska sojourns, they brought with them mouth watering memories of outdoor Alaskan salmon barbecues. This recipe brings thoughts of Alaska to them and delicious eating to all of us.

2   tablespoons margarine or butter, melted
2   tablespoons brown sugar
2   tablespoons lemon juice
½   teaspoon dried dill weed
4   [1-inch thick] salmon steaks

1. In small dish, combine melted margarine, brown sugar, lemon juice and dill weed.

2. Coat grill or punctured foil with oil.

3. Place salmon steaks on prepared surface.

4. Grill slowly over ash covered coals, about 10-15 minutes.

5. Brush frequently with sauce.

6. Turn once and cook approximately 10 minutes more until salmon flakes when fork tested.

BARBECUED HALIBUT STEAKS

[Serves 4-6]

As cooking fish on the grill has become popular, there is a need for flavorful marinades. Look no further. Here is a delicious winner using ingredients that most cooks have on hand.

½   cup soy sauce
¼   cup ketchup
½   cup orange juice
2   tablespoons lemon juice
¼   cup minced fresh parsley
¼   teaspoon garlic powder
¼   teaspoon ground pepper
2   lbs. halibut or other fish steaks, cut about 1-inch thick

[continued]

BARBECUED HALIBUT STEAKS [continued]

1. Combine soy sauce, ketchup, orange juice, lemon juice, parsley, garlic powder and pepper.

2. Put halibut in shallow dish or resealable plastic bag. Pour marinade over halibut, turning fish to cover evenly with marinade.

3. Marinate one hour in the refrigerator.

4. Position grill about 4 inches from hot coals.

5. Remove halibut from marinade and put on grill that has been oiled or covered with foil that has been punctured.

6. Grill for about 15 minutes, turning once.

7. Baste frequently with marinade.

PUMPERNICKEL HAM MELTS

[Serves 2]

Whether you use the extra ham from Sunday dinner or purchase slices from the deli counter, this is a lightning quick entree. Add fresh fruit and tall glasses of milk to complete a nutritious menu.

2   slices pumpernickel bread, toasted
2   teaspoons Dijon mustard
¼   pound thinly sliced ham
½   cup fresh alfalfa sprouts
½   small onion, thinly sliced and separated into rings
½   cup shredded mozzarella cheese

1. Spread mustard on one side of each bread slice.

2. Top each slice with half the ham, alfalfa sprouts, onion and cheese.

3. Broil sandwiches 4 to 6 inches from heat for 2 to 3 minutes or until hot and cheese is melted.

Microwave

In step 3, place sandwiches on double layer of paper towel. Microwave on 100% power 2 to 4 minutes or until hot and cheese is melted, rotating sandwiches once.

TURKEY PROVOLONE HERO

[Serves 8-10]

A hero sandwich is described as a large sandwich filled with meats, cheeses and accompaniments. This recipe gives the basic plan....vary the ingredient list depending on availability and personal choice.

1   [3 ounce] package cream cheese, softened
2   tablespoons light or regular sour cream
2   teaspoons Dijon mustard
½   teaspoon prepared horseradish
1   [16 ounce] loaf Vienna or Italian bread
    Fresh spinach leaves
½   pound thinly sliced cooked turkey
6   ounces thinly sliced provolone cheese
2   medium tomatoes, sliced
1   cup alfalfa sprouts

1. In small mixing bowl, mix together cream cheese, sour cream, mustard and horseradish. Set aside.

2. Cut bread in half lengthwise.

3. Spread cut sides of bread with mustard spread.

4. On bottom half of loaf, layer spinach, turkey, cheese, tomato and sprouts.

5. Replace top half of loaf. Hold together with long frilly toothpicks, if desired.

6. At serving time, slice into individual servings.

Roast Beef Barbecues

[Serves 15]

This easy to prepare, crowd pleasing recipe is packed with great flavor. I often use roast beef from the deli, but meat from a cooked roast works equally well. Efficient cooks will want to prepare the recipe ahead of time and then bake just before serving.

1	tablespoon vegetable oil
1	large onion, thinly sliced
⅜	teaspoon garlic powder
⅓	cup brown sugar
¾	cup prepared steak sauce
3	[8 ounce] cans tomato sauce
2	pounds cooked beef, thinly sliced
15	sandwich buns, toasted, if desired

1. Heat oil over medium-high heat in large skillet.

2. Add onion and garlic powder; cook and stir until tender.

3. Stir in brown sugar, steak sauce and tomato sauce; bring to a boil. Reduce heat. Cover; simmer 15 minutes.

4. Place beef in large 3-4 quart flat casserole; add sauce and stir to combine.

5. Cover; bake in preheated 325 degree oven for 1 to 1¼ hours or until flavors are blended.

6. To serve, spoon about ½ cup barbecue mixture on each bun.

Microwave

In step 1, omit oil.

In step 2, put onion, garlic powder, and 1 tablespoon water in 2 quart microwave-safe casserole. Cover with lid or vented plastic wrap. Microwave on 100% power 2-3 minutes, until onion is tender, stirring once.

In step 3, stir in brown sugar, steak sauce and tomato sauce. Microwave on 100% power 4-6 minutes until mixture boils, stirring once or twice. Microwave an additional 10-12 minutes at 80% power, stirring twice.

PICNIC TORTILLA ROLL-UPS

[Serves 8-10]

This quick and easy "sandwich" idea is both fun to make and fun to eat. That's why they are designed for a picnic or any other quick and casual meal. Join the fun and try this recipe soon.

½   **cup light or regular sour cream**
¼   **cup light or regular mayonnaise or salad dressing**
3   **tablespoons salsa or picante sauce, mild, medium or hot**
10   **[6-8 inch] flour tortillas**
10   **thin slices deli style roast beef, turkey, or ham**
10   **large lettuce leaves, washed and dried**
     Toothpicks, with frills if desired

1. In small mixing bowl, mix together sour cream, mayonnaise and salsa or picante sauce.

2. To separate tortillas, warm according to package directions, if desired.

3. Spread sour cream mixture on tortillas.

4. Arrange meat and lettuce on tortillas.

5. Roll tortillas, jelly roll fashion; secure with a wooden toothpick.

6. Wrap in plastic wrap to take to a picnic or arrange on serving platter.

Open-Faced Crab Delights

[Serves 2 or 3]

Open-faced sandwiches just seem to have a special pizazz about them. So it's easy to understand why this whole wheat crab combination is a popular light entree. Chopping the imitation crab in a food processor ensures an even desirable texture.

2   tablespoons chopped green pepper
2   tablespoons chopped onion
¼   cup light mayonnaise
1   teaspoon lemon juice
    Dash of pepper
1   [6 ounce] package frozen imitation crab, thawed & chopped
3   slices whole wheat bread, toasted
½   cup shredded light or regular Cheddar cheese
    Fresh parsley for garnish, if desired

1. In mixing bowl, combine green pepper, onion, mayonnaise, lemon juice and pepper; mix well.

2. Gently stir in chopped crab.

3. Spread ½ cup mixture on each slice of toast; sprinkle with cheese.

4. Broil 5 inches from heat for 2 to 3 minutes or until cheese melts and mixture is thoroughly heated.

5. Garnish with parsley, if desired.

DILLY TUNA BROCCOLI SALAD

[Serves 6-8]

Vitamin packed broccoli adds a colorful crunchy texture as well as excellent nutrition to this clever tuna salad idea. The delicious dill dressing gently binds all the ingredients together in a special way.

2   [6½ ounce] cans water-packed tuna, drained, flaked
2   cups chopped fresh broccoli flowerets
¼   cup chopped onion
½   cup chopped celery
1   [8 ounce] can sliced water chestnuts, drained
1   [8 ounce] can bamboo shoots, drained
1   cup light or regular mayonnaise
1   tablespoon lemon juice
1   teaspoon dill weed
⅛   teaspoon pepper
    Sunflower kernels for garnish, if desired

1. In large bowl, combine tuna, broccoli, onion, celery, water chestnuts and bamboo shoots. Toss gently to combine.

2. In small bowl, combine mayonnaise, lemon juice, dill weed and pepper. Whisk together to evenly combine.

3. Pour dressing over tuna mixture. Mix well.

4. Refrigerate several hours to blend flavors.

5. Garnish with sunflower kernels, if desired.

CRABMEAT SALAD

[Serves 4]

This exciting crabmeat salad is a favorite light lunch of my brother-in-law, Ross House. The rice stick noodles, found in the Oriental foods section at the super market, literally "explode" when they cook. This noodle cooking experience is so much fun, you'll want to make this delicious salad again and again.

¼   cup water
¼   cup white vinegar
¼   cup sugar
½   teaspoon salt
2   teaspoons finely chopped garlic
1   tablespoon sesame seed oil
     Vegetable oil
2   ounces or a small handful of rice stick noodles
3   cups shredded iceberg lettuce
6-8 ounces crabmeat or imitation crab
2   tablespoons chopped green onions, with tops
1   tablespoon toasted sesame seeds

1. In small saucepan, heat water, vinegar, sugar and salt to boiling over medium heat. Cook, uncovered, 5 minutes; cool.

2. Stir in garlic and sesame oil. Cover and refrigerate dressing.

3. Heat oil to 425 degrees. Pull noodles apart and fry about ¼ at a time, about 5 seconds until puffed. Drain on paper towels.

4. Toss lettuce and crabmeat with dressing until evenly coated. Let stand 5 minutes. Drain.

5. In large salad bowl, combine drained lettuce and crabmeat with rice noodles, green onion and sesame seeds; Toss.

6. Serve immediately.

Microwave

In step **1**, measure water, vinegar, sugar and salt in 1 quart microwave-safe measurer. Microwave on 100% power 1-2 minutes, until boiling, stirring once. Continue to microwave on 100% power 3-4 minutes; cool.

SWISS TURKEY SALAD

[Serves 8]

Layered vegetable salads are popular on the "pot luck" or "pitch in" dinner circuit. Add the extra punch of protein from cooked turkey and you have one terrific totable entree.

4   cups torn iceberg lettuce
1   [10 ounce] package frozen peas, thawed and drained
1   [8 ounce] can sliced water chestnuts, drained
1   cup chopped celery
½   cup chopped onion
½   cup chopped green pepper
3   cups coarsely chopped cooked turkey
1½ cups light or regular mayonnaise
1   tablespoon sugar
1½ cups shredded Swiss cheese [6 ounces]
8   slices bacon, cooked and crumbled

1. In 9x13 inch pan or other large flat dish, layer the lettuce, peas, water chestnuts, celery, onion, green pepper and turkey, beginning with lettuce in the order listed.

2. Combine mayonnaise and sugar. Gently spread mixture over turkey.

3. Top with cheese and bacon.

4. Cover tightly; chill.

5. Serve and enjoy.

Accompaniments

In the corporate world, this chapter of accompaniments would be known as support staff. Breads, salads and vegetables undergird entrees creating a winning menu.

Variety adds interest to meals, so you will find an array of both quick and yeast breads as well as a grand selection of fruit and vegetable salads. Finally, this grouping includes vibrant cooked vegetable ideas complete with several ways to serve rice.

Do add these significant recipes to your repertoire.

Contents

APPLE COFFEE CAKE

[Serves 8-10]

This delicious coffee cake uses ingredients that most folks keep on hand. You'll find a double layer of cinnamon sugared apple slices that assures full flavor in every bite.

½   **cup light brown sugar**
2   **tablespoons flour**
1   **teaspoon cinnamon**
2   **tablespoons margarine or butter**
½   **cup sugar**
¼   **cup margarine or butter, softened**
1   **egg**
½   **cup milk**
1½ **cups flour**
2   **teaspoons baking powder**
½   **teaspoon salt**
2   **cups apples, pared, thinly sliced**

1. In small bowl, combine brown sugar, 2 tablespoons flour, and cinnamon. Cut in 2 tablespoons margarine until mixture is crumbly. Set aside.

2. In medium bowl, cream together sugar and ¼ cup margarine.

3. Add egg and beat well.

4. Stir in milk.

5. Sift together flour, baking powder and salt; stir into egg mixture just until smooth.

6. Spread half of the batter in greased 8x8-inch baking pan.

7. Cover with half the apples and half the brown sugar mixture.

8. Repeat layers.

9. Bake in preheated 375 degree oven for 45-50 minutes or until toothpick inserted in cake portion comes out clean.

BLUEBERRY COFFEE CAKE

[Serves 12-16]

This wonderful family-sized coffee cake reminds me of row upon row of hearty blueberries that grow here in Southwest Michigan. Whether you make a trip to the U-pick blueberry patch or select them at the grocery store, blueberries are a fruit to treasure.

½   cup margarine or butter, softened
1   cup sugar
1   teaspoon vanilla
3   eggs
1   cup light or regular sour cream
2   cups flour
1   teaspoon baking soda
1   teaspoon salt
2   cups fresh blueberries
1   cup brown sugar
1   cup chopped walnuts or pecans
1   teaspoon cinnamon

1. In mixing bowl, beat margarine, sugar and vanilla until light and fluffy, with an electric mixer.

2. Add eggs, one at a time, beating well after each addition. Beat in sour cream.

3. Sift together flour, soda and salt. Add to creamed mixture and beat well.

4. By hand, fold in blueberries. Set aside.

5. In small bowl, combine brown sugar, nuts and cinnamon.

6. Spread half of the batter in greased 9x13 inch baking pan. Sprinkle half of the brown sugar mixture evenly over batter.

7. Dollop remaining batter on top; gently spread batter.

8. Sprinkle remaining brown sugar mixture over surface of batter.

9. Bake in preheated 350 degree oven for 45-50 minutes or until done.

ZUCCHINI SPICE COFFEE CAKE

[Serves 12]

Warm from the oven or baked ahead of time, moist squares of this humble coffee cake will welcome morning in proper style. In all honesty, it's a great midnight snack too.

½   cup margarine or butter, softened
¼   cup dairy sour cream
1   cup brown sugar
2   eggs
1   teaspoon vanilla
1½ cups flour
1   teaspoon baking soda
1   teaspoon cinnamon
½   teaspoon salt
¼   teaspoon nutmeg
1¼ cups quick cooking rolled oats
2   cups shredded zucchini

TOPPING:

¾   cup sugar
½   cup flour
½   cup quick cooking rolled oats
½   teaspoon cinnamon
¼   cup margarine or butter, softened

1. In large mixing bowl, cream together ½ cup margarine, sour cream, and brown sugar until thoroughly mixed.

2. Beat in eggs, one at a time. Stir in vanilla.

3. Sift together the 1½ cups flour, baking soda, 1 teaspoon cinnamon, salt, and nutmeg.

4. Stir dry ingredients into creamed mixture.

5. Stir in 1¼ cups quick oats.

6. Add zucchini. Fold gently until evenly combined.

7. Pour into greased 9x13 inch baking pan.

[continued]

ZUCCHINI SPICE COFFEE CAKE [continued]

8. In small bowl, combine sugar, ½ cup flour, ½ cup quick oats, ½ teaspoon cinnamon and ¼ cup margarine.

9. Mix until crumbly; sprinkle over batter.

10. Bake in preheated 350 degree oven 30-40 minutes or until toothpick inserted in center comes out clean.

11. Cut into squares; serve warm or cooled.

ORANGE RHUBARB COFFEE CAKE

[Serves 9-12]

Simply scrumptious aptly describes this mouth watering coffee cake. Both the ingredient list and procedure are simple, but the outstanding flavor could easily seem complicated.

¼ **cup margarine or butter, softened**
¾ **cup sugar**
1 **egg**
½ **cup orange juice**
1¼ **cups flour**
1½ **teaspoons baking powder**
¼ **teaspoon salt**
2 **teaspoons grated orange rind**
1½ **cups chopped fresh or frozen rhubarb**

TOPPING:

2 **tablespoons sugar**
½ **teaspoon cinnamon**

1. In mixing bowl, cream margarine and ¾ cup sugar until light and fluffy.

2. Beat in egg and orange juice.

3. Sift together flour, baking powder and salt. Stir into creamed mixture.

4. Add orange rind and rhubarb. Mix well.

5. Pour into greased and floured 9 inch square pan.

6. Combine 2 tablespoons sugar and cinnamon; sprinkle over cake.

7. Bake in preheated 350 degree oven 35-40 minutes or until toothpick inserted in center comes out clean.

BLUEBERRY PANCAKES

[Makes 8 [4 inch] pancakes]

Summertime is blueberry time here in southwest Michigan. We enjoy them morning, noon and night. So start the day with these quick and easy blueberry pancakes. Oh yes, these pancakes are so popular, you may need to double the recipe.

1	cup flour
1½	teaspoons baking powder
½	teaspoon salt
1	tablespoon sugar
¼	teaspoon ground cinnamon
1	egg, separated
2	tablespoons margarine or butter, melted
¾	cup milk
¾	cup fresh or frozen blueberries

1. Combine flour, baking powder, salt, sugar and cinnamon in mixing bowl.

2. Beat egg yolk until thick and lemon colored; add melted margarine and milk, stirring until blended.

3. Add liquid mixture to dry ingredients, stirring just until moistened.

4. Beat egg white until stiff peaks form; fold into batter.

5. Gently fold in blueberries

6. For each pancake, pour about ¼ cup batter onto a hot, lightly greased griddle.

7. Turn pancakes when center bubbles form and edges look cooked.

8. Enjoy with your favorite syrup.

BEEHIVE BROWN BREAD

[Makes 3 loaves]

It was a great day when June Carlson shared this bread recipe with students in a Portage Community Education class. Reminiscent of Boston Brown Bread, you'll find no oil or eggs in the heart smart ingredient list.

3	cups whole wheat flour
1	cup flour
1	cup sugar
1½	teaspoons baking soda
½	teaspoon salt, if desired
1	cup raisins
1	cup lowfat buttermilk
1	cup skim milk
1	cup water
1	cup molasses

1. In large mixing bowl, combine whole wheat flour, flour, sugar, soda, and salt. Stir to thoroughly combine.

2. Toss raisins in flour mixture.

3. Add buttermilk, milk, water and molasses to flour mixture. Mix well.

4. Pour batter into three well-greased 1 pound coffee cans or other round cans, filling no more than ¾ full of batter.

5. Bake in preheated 350 degree oven 50-60 minutes or till wooden pick comes out clean.

6. Cool bread in cans 10-15 minutes before removing bread from can.

7. Cool on wire rack.

8. Store well wrapped in refrigerator.

CHOCOLATE BREAD

[Makes 1 loaf]

Chocolate lovers will cheer when you serve this mouth watering bread. We like to toast it for an early morning treat.

½	cup margarine or butter, softened
1	cup sugar
2	eggs
1	cup buttermilk
1¾	cups flour
½	cup unsweetened cocoa
½	teaspoon baking powder
½	teaspoon baking soda
½	teaspoon salt
½	cup chopped walnuts or pecans

1. In large mixing bowl, cream together margarine and sugar.

2. Add eggs, one at a time, beating well after each addition.

3. Stir in buttermilk.

4. Sift together flour, cocoa, baking powder, baking soda, and salt. Stir into creamed mixture until dry particles are moistened.

5. Stir in nuts.

6. Pour into well greased 8x4 inch baking pan.

7. Bake in preheated 350 degree oven 55-65 minutes or until wooden pick comes out clean.

8. Cool in pan 10 minutes. Remove from pan and cool completely on wire rack.

CHOCOLATE CHIP-BANANA BREAD

[Makes 1 loaf]

Miniature chocolate chips push this banana bread right into the grand championship category. What a great way to use those last two extra ripe bananas.

½   **cup margarine or butter, softened**
1   **cup sugar**
2   **eggs**
2   **ripe bananas, mashed**
2   **cups flour**
1   **teaspoon baking powder**
½   **teaspoon baking soda**
½   **teaspoon salt**
¾   **cup semisweet chocolate mini-morsels**
½   **cup chopped walnuts or pecans**

1. Cream margarine with sugar until thoroughly blended.

2. Add eggs, one at a time, beating after each addition.

3. Stir in mashed bananas.

4. Sift together flour, baking powder, baking soda and salt.

5. Add sifted ingredients to creamed mixture and stir until flour is evenly distributed.

6. Stir in chocolate mini-morsels and walnuts or pecans.

7. Spoon batter into a well greased 9x5 inch loaf pan.

8. Bake in preheated 350 degree oven 60-70 minutes or until a wooden pick inserted in center comes out clean, shielding with aluminum foil after 1 hour, if necessary.

9. Cool in pan 10 minutes; remove from pan, and cool completely on wire rack.

PUMPKIN CHOCOLATE CHIP BREAD

[Makes 1 loaf]

Just when you think it's traditional pumpkin bread, the chocolate chips get your attention. Here's a quick bread that could even double as dessert.

½   cup margarine or butter, softened
1   cup sugar
2   eggs
1¾ cups flour
1   teaspoon baking soda
½   teaspoon salt
½   teaspoon ground cinnamon
½   teaspoon ground nutmeg
¼   teaspoon ground ginger
¼   teaspoon ground cloves
¾   cup mashed cooked pumpkin
¾   cup semisweet chocolate morsels
¾   cup chopped pecans, divided

1. Cream together margarine and sugar.

2. Add eggs, one at a time, beating well after each addition.

3. Sift together flour, soda, salt, cinnamon, nutmeg, ginger and cloves.

4. Add flour mixture to creamed mixture alternately with pumpkin, beginning and ending with flour mixture.

5. Stir in chocolate morsels and ½ cup pecans.

6. Spoon mixture into a greased and parchment lined or floured 9x5 inch baking pan.

7. Sprinkle batter with remaining ¼ cup pecans.

8. Bake in preheated 350 degree oven 60-70 minutes or until wooden pick inserted in center comes out clean.

9. Cool bread in pan 10 minutes, remove from pan.

10. Continue cooling on wire rack.

IRISH SODA BREAD

[Makes 1 loaf]

Every March I get in the mood for this traditional bread when I prepare a Corned Beef and Cabbage dinner in honor of St. Patrick's Day. Raisins and caraway seeds give this loaf its interesting old world flavor.

4	**cups flour**
¼	**cup sugar**
1	**teaspoon salt**
1	**teaspoon baking powder**
2	**tablespoons caraway seeds**
¼	**cup margarine or butter**
2	**cups raisins**
1⅓	**cups buttermilk**
1	**egg**
1	**teaspoon baking soda**
1	**egg yolk, beaten**

1. Sift flour, sugar, salt and baking powder into mixing bowl; stir in caraway seeds.

2. Cut in margarine until mixture looks like coarse meal; stir in raisins.

3. Combine buttermilk, 1 egg, and baking soda; stir into flour mixture just enough to moisten dry ingredients.

4. Turn dough onto floured board and knead lightly until dough is smooth. Shape in a ball and place in a greased 2-quart casserole.

5. With sharp knife, cut a 4 inch cross about ½ inch deep in center of dough to make a decorative top.

6. Brush with egg yolk.

7. Bake in preheated 375 degree oven about 1 hour, or until a wooden pick inserted in center of loaf comes out clean.

8. Cool bread in casserole 10 minutes; remove.

9. Cool on wire rack before cutting.

10. To serve, cut down through loaf to divide in quarters; thinly slice each quarter.

APRICOT-BRAN MUFFINS

[Makes 1 dozen]

Apricot enthusiasts will thank you again and again when they taste these wonderful bran muffins. How fortunate I am that my friend, Mary Reineke, shared this recipe which had come from her son-in-law, Bill Lyth.

1½ cups all bran cereal
1   cup buttermilk
1   egg
¼   cup vegetable oil
6   tablespoons brown sugar
1   cup flour
1   teaspoon baking soda
¼   teaspoon salt, if desired
1   cup chopped dried apricots

1. In medium mixing bowl, combine all bran cereal and buttermilk. Let stand for a few minutes to soften bran.

2. Stir in egg, oil and brown sugar. Mix well.

3. Sift together flour, baking soda and salt.

4. Add dry ingredients, stirring just until flour disappears.

5. Gently stir in apricots.

6. Fill lightly greased muffin cups ¾ full with batter.

7. Bake in preheated 400 degree oven 15 minutes or until muffins are lightly browned.

RICH'S FAVORITE RAISIN BRAN MUFFINS

[Makes 18-24 muffins]

My brother, Rich Howell who lives in Dallas, Texas, likes to bake these raisin filled muffins. When I questioned him about the ¼ cup milk in addition to the buttermilk, Rich told me that he uses that milk to rinse out the buttermilk measuring cup. Do you suppose cooking tips run in our genes?

2	cups buttermilk
¼	cup milk
2	eggs, beaten
½	cup vegetable oil
2½	cups flour
½	cup sugar
2½	teaspoons baking soda
1	teaspoon salt
4	cups raisin bran cereal
1	cup raisins

1. In large mixing bowl, combine buttermilk, milk, eggs and oil. Mix well.

2. Add flour, sugar, soda and salt. Stir until all dry ingredients disappear.

3. Stir in raisin bran cereal and raisins.

4. Fill greased muffin cups ¾ full.

5. Bake in preheated 400 degree oven 15-20 minutes or until lightly browned.

Tip:

Batter may be stored in tightly covered container in refrigerator up to 1 week.

OAT BRAN MUFFINS

[Makes 12]

Several years ago when the virtues of oat bran received publicity for helping to lower cholesterol levels, I found this moist raisin-filled muffin recipe. If you're a heart healthy cook, this idea is certain to become part of your permanent recipe file.

2½ cups oat bran
½ cup raisins
1 tablespoon brown sugar
1 tablespoon baking powder
⅛ teaspoon salt
½ cup unsweetened applesauce
1 cup skim milk
½ cup egg substitute or 2 egg whites
1 tablespoon vegetable oil
 Vegetable cooking spray

1. Combine oat bran, raisins, brown sugar, baking powder, and salt in a large mixing bowl; make a well in center of mixture.

2. Combine applesauce, milk, egg substitute and oil, stirring well.

3. Add applesauce mixture into well of dry ingredients, stirring just until moistened.

4. Coat muffin pans or paper baking cups with cooking spray.

5. Spoon batter into pans, filling quite full.

6. Bake in preheated 425 degree oven for 20-25 minutes or until golden.

BLUEBERRY CAKE MUFFINS

[Makes 18]

Many Michigan Blueberry Muffin lovers are partial to the tender cake-like texture of these muffins. Tuck extra muffins in the freezer for a special treat some "blue day".

½   **cup margarine or butter, softened**
¾   **cup sugar**
2   **eggs**
1   **teaspoon vanilla**
2   **cups flour**
1½ **teaspoons baking powder**
¼   **teaspoon salt**
½   **cup milk**
1½ **cups fresh or frozen blueberries**

1. Cream together margarine and sugar. Beat in eggs one at a time. Stir in vanilla.

2. Sift together flour, baking powder, and salt.

3. Add flour mixture alternately with milk, beginning and ending with flour. Stir just until smooth.

4. Gently fold in blueberries.

5. Fill paper lined or greased muffin cups ⅔ full of batter.

6. Bake in preheated 375 degree oven 25-30 minutes or until lightly browned.

DATE-NUT MUFFINS

[Makes 10]

Whenever I find a few dates lurking in the refrigerator, I'm reminded of these tender sweet muffins. Remember, muffins are a thoughtful addition to luncheon and supper menus as well as breakfasts and brunches.

1½ cups flour
½ cup sugar
2 teaspoons baking powder
½ teaspoon salt
¾ cup chopped dates
½ cup chopped pecans or walnuts
1 egg, beaten
½ cup milk
¼ cup margarine or butter, melted

1. In medium mixing bowl, sift together flour, sugar, baking powder and salt.

2. Stir in dates and nuts. Make a well in the center.

3. Combine egg, milk and melted margarine.

4. Pour liquid ingredients into well in dry mixture.

5. Stir just until flour disappears.

6. Spoon into greased muffin pans, filling ¾ full.

7. Bake in preheated 400 degree oven 18-20 minutes or until muffins are lightly browned.

OATMEAL APPLESAUCE MUFFINS

[Makes 12 muffins]

It was a "Heart Smart" day when I received this muffin recipe from Mary Ellen Overbeek who lives near Scotts, Michigan. She says the recipe was actually developed by her friend, Stephanie Vander Straaten, and now lots of people are baking these healthy muffins.

½   cup flour
¾   cup whole wheat flour
½   cup brown sugar
1   cup quick cooking uncooked oats
½   teaspoon baking powder
½   teaspoon baking soda
1   teaspoon cinnamon
1   egg white
1   cup skim milk
½   cup applesauce

1. In medium mixing bowl, combine flour, whole wheat flour, brown sugar, oats, baking powder, baking soda, and cinnamon. Mix thoroughly and make a "well" in the center.

2. Put egg white, milk and applesauce in "well". Mix well.

3. Spray muffin pans with vegetable spray.

4. Fill muffin cups with batter.

5. Bake in preheated 400 degree oven 15-20 minutes or until lightly browned.

MINI PUMPKIN MUFFINS

[Makes 36 mini-muffins]

Whenever a dainty bread product is part of a menu plan, small bite size muffins are the perfect suggestion. This pumpkin variation is especially welcome during the autumn months.

¼ **cup shortening**
⅔ **cup sugar**
1 **egg**
1 **cup flour**
2 **teaspoons baking powder**
¼ **teaspoon salt**
¼ **teaspoon ground cinnamon**
½ **cup canned mashed pumpkin**
2 **tablespoons milk**
½ **cup raisins, if desired**

1. Cream together shortening and sugar in mixing bowl until light and fluffy, using the electric mixer at medium speed

2. Beat in egg.

3. Sift together flour, baking powder, salt and cinnamon; set aside.

4. In small bowl, combine pumpkin and milk.

5. Add dry ingredients alternately with pumpkin mixture to creamed mixture, beginning and ending with dry ingredients. Stir well after each addition. Add raisins, if desired.

6. Fill paper lined miniature muffin cups ¾ full of batter.

7. Bake in preheated 350 degree oven 15-20 minutes or until golden brown.

HONEY WHOLE WHEAT BREAD

[Makes 2 loaves]

On a day when you feel like baking bread, try this moist flavorful wheat bread. My husband, George, thinks it's one of the best yeast breads he has ever tasted.

2   **packages active dry yeast**
½   **cup warm water [105-115 degrees]**
1   **egg**
¾   **cup honey**
½   **cup nonfat dry milk powder**
1   **tablespoon salt**
2   **tablespoons vegetable oil**
1¾ **cups warm water [105-115 degrees]**
3   **cups whole wheat flour**
4 -4 ½ **cups flour**

1. Dissolve yeast in ½ cup warm water in large mixing bowl; let stand 5 minutes.

2. To yeast mixture, add egg, honey, nonfat dry milk powder, salt, vegetable oil and warm water. Beat with electric mixer until well combined.

3. Add whole wheat flour; beat at medium speed of an electric mixer until smooth.

4. Stir in enough flour to make a stiff dough.

5. Turn dough out on a floured surface, and knead until smooth and elastic.

6. Put dough into bowl. Cover with oiled plastic wrap and let rise in a warm place until dough has doubled in bulk.

7. Punch dough down; divide in half, and shape into two loaves.

8. Place dough in two well-greased 8x4 inch loaf pans; cover with oiled plastic wrap and let rise until double in bulk.

9. Uncover and bake in preheated 375 degree oven for 30 minutes or until loaves sound hollow when tapped, shielding loaves with aluminum foil, if necessary, to prevent overbrowning.

Mary Ellen's Sourdough Chowder Buns

[Makes 4 or 6]

For years I've been wanting to make yeast bread soup bowls. So, I was thrilled when my friend, Mary Ellen Behm, shared this great recipe with me. Even though the sourdough starter needs to be made ahead of time, the entire procedure is actually very easy.

½	cup warm water [105-115 degrees]
1	package active dry yeast
5	cups flour
3	tablespoons sugar
1	tablespoon salt
1	egg, beaten
1	cup sourdough starter, [recipe below]
1	cup warm water [105-115 degrees]
3	tablespoons vegetable oil

1. Dissolve yeast in ½ cup warm water. Set aside.

2. In large mixing bowl, combine flour, sugar and salt. Make a well in the center of the dry ingredients and set aside.

3. In medium mixing bowl, combine dissolved yeast, beaten egg, sourdough starter, water and oil. Mix thoroughly.

4. Pour liquid ingredients into well in dry ingredients.

5. Stir with wooden spoon until a soft, sticky dough is formed.

6. Cover bowl with oiled plastic wrap and set in a warm place until the dough doubles in bulk.

7. Punch down dough. Divide into 4 or 6 pieces.

8. Flour cut sides and pat out on floured surface with finger tips. Form into a large bun with smooth surface.

9. Place on greased or parchment lined cookie sheets, leaving 2-3 inches between buns. Cover with oiled plastic wrap. Let rise until double in bulk.

10. Bake in preheated 350 degree oven for 35-40 minutes. Cool.

11. Just before serving, slice off top and hollow out bun so it can be used as a bowl. Save bread from hollowing out the buns.

[continued]

MARY ELLEN'S SOURDOUGH CHOWDER BUNS [continued]

12. Serve your favorite chowder or thick soup or stew in "bun bowls". Serve the leftover bread from hollowing out the buns on the plate with the chowder.

SOURDOUGH STARTER:

2 cups flour
1 package active dry yeast
1½ cups warm water [105-115 degrees]

1. In large bowl, combine flour and dry yeast.

2. Add water to make a thick batter. Mix thoroughly.

3. Let stand, covered, in a warm place for at least 24 hours.

4. Store sourdough starter in refrigerator in a tightly covered bowl large enough to allow for expansion of starter.

To Keep Sourdough Starter Alive:

1. The sourdough starter must be fed at least every 8 days or it will "die"

2. Sourdough starter my be frozen. If frozen, thaw, and use the day after it is fed.

3. To feed Sourdough Starter: Mix together 1 cup flour, ½ cup sugar and 1 cup milk.

4. Add mixture to starter left in bowl and let sit at room temperature until it begins to bubble. Then cover and refrigerate.

5. Do not use starter the same day it is fed.

6. It's a good idea to have the sourdough starter at room temperature when it's used in a recipe.

RAISIN BREAD

[Makes 2 loaves]

Sometimes when things get stressful, baking yeast bread is a great therapeutic idea. Permit me to suggest this outstanding raisin bread recipe. It's a real winner.

2	**cups milk**
⅔	**cup sugar**
2	**tablespoons margarine or butter**
1	**teaspoon salt**
2	**packages active dry yeast**
½	**cup warm water [105-115 degrees]**
1	**egg**
1	**teaspoon ground cinnamon**
8	**cups flour**
1	**cup raisins**

1. Scald milk in saucepan.

2. In large mixing bowl, combine hot milk, sugar, margarine and salt. Cool to lukewarm.

3. Sprinkle yeast over warm water; stir to dissolve.

4. Add yeast mixture, egg, cinnamon and 4 cups of the flour to milk mixture. Beat with electric mixer at medium speed until smooth, about 2 minutes. Stir in raisins.

5. Gradually stir in enough remaining flour to make a stiff dough.

6. Turn dough onto floured surface. Knead until smooth.

7. Place dough in greased bowl, turning over once to grease top. Cover with oiled plastic wrap and let rise in warm place until doubled.

8. Punch down dough. Divide dough in half. Let rest 10 minutes.

9. Shape each half into a loaf. Place in 2 greased 9x5 inch loaf pans.

10. Cover with oiled plastic wrap and let rise until doubled.

11. Bake in preheated 350 degree oven 40 minutes, or until loaves sound hollow when tapped.

12. Remove from pan; cool on racks.

SOUR CREAM CRESCENT ROLLS

[Makes 2 dozen rolls]

Our Texas niece, Christina Howell, really enjoys these light delicate rolls, so I try to have the dough waiting in the refrigerator when she comes for a visit to Michigan. That way we can have hot rolls from the oven on very short notice.

¼   **cup margarine or butter**
½   **cup light or regular sour cream**
¼   **cup sugar**
½   **teaspoon salt**
1   **package dry yeast**
¼   **cup warm water [105 to 115 degrees]**
1   **egg**
2   **cups flour**
1   **egg white, slightly beaten**

1. Combine margarine, sour cream, sugar and salt in small saucepan. Cook over low heat until margarine melts. Cool to 105-115 degrees.

2. Dissolve yeast in warm water in a large mixing bowl; let stand 5 minutes.

3. Beat egg and sour cream mixture into dissolved yeast.

4. Beat in 1 cup flour.

5. Stir in remaining cup of flour, mixing well.

6. Cover tightly and refrigerate 8-24 hours.

7. Punch dough down, and divide in half. Roll each portion in a 12 inch circle on a floured surface.

8. Cut each circle into 12 wedges; roll each wedge, jelly roll fashion, beginning at wide end.

9. Place on greased or parchment lined baking sheets, point side down.

10. Cover with oiled plastic wrap and let rise in warm place until doubled in bulk.

11. Brush with egg white.

12. Bake in preheated 375 degree oven 12-15 minutes or until rolls are golden brown.

DAWN'S LOVELY YEAST DOUGH

[Makes 2 medium coffee cakes or 3-4 dozen rolls]

Dawn Andrew, who lives near the Howell family farm in southern Wisconsin, is a talented yeast bread baker who generously shares her efforts with family and friends. Many a breakfast menu back home on the farm has been highlighted by a mouth watering coffee cake she baked and delivered that very morning.

1½ **cups milk**
½ **cup margarine or butter**
½ **cup sugar**
1 **teaspoon salt**
½ **cup warm water [105-115 degrees]**
2 **packages active dry yeast**
2 **eggs, beaten**
6½ -7 **cups flour**

1. Place milk and margarine in saucepan. Heat to scalding. Pour into large mixing bowl. Add sugar and salt. Stir to dissolve. Cool until lukewarm.

2. Meanwhile, dissolve yeast in lukewarm water in 1 cup glass measurer.

3. To lukewarm milk mixture, add 1½ cups flour. Beat until smooth.

4. Add eggs and ½ cup more flour. Beat well.

5. Add dissolved yeast and 2 more cups flour. Beat well.

6. Stir in 2½ cups flour to make a soft dough.

7. Using as much of the ½ cup remaining flour as required, knead until smooth.

8. Place in greased bowl. Cover with oiled plastic wrap. Let rise in warm draft-free place until double in bulk.

9. Punch down dough. Let rise a second time until double in bulk.

10. Punch down dough again. Shape in desired roll shapes or roll into a circle and fill for a coffee cake.

11. Cover with oiled plastic wrap. Let rolls or coffee cake rise double in size.

12. Bake in preheated 375 degree oven 15-20 minutes or until golden brown. Brush with melted butter and remove to racks to cool.

[continued]

Dawn's Lovely Yeast Dough [continued]

Microwave

In step **1**, microwave milk in large microwave-safe mixing bowl on 100% power 3-4 minutes.

In step **2**, probe water for yeast to 110 degrees.

Dawn's Coffee Cake

2 **tablespoons softened margarine or butter**
½ **cup brown sugar**
2 **teaspoons cinnamon**
½ **cup raisins**

1. In step **10**, divide dough in half. Roll each half into a 9x15 inch rectangle. Spread dough with margarine or butter. Sprinkle with brown sugar and cinnamon. Sprinkle with raisins, if desired.

2. Roll up, beginning at wide side. Pinch edge of dough into roll to seal well. Stretch roll to make even.

3. With sealed edge down, shape into ring on parchment lined or lightly greased baking sheet. Pinch ends together. With scissors, make cuts ⅔ of the way through ring at 1 inch intervals. Turn each section on its side. Cover with oiled plastic wrap. Let rise until double in size.

4. Repeat procedure with other half of dough.

5. After coffee cake is baked and cooled, drizzle with Confectioners' Sugar Icing, if desired.

OATMEAL SQUASH BREAD

[Makes 2 loaves]

Winter squash improves the flavor, texture and keeping qualities of this unique yeast bread. I find both butternut or buttercup squash work very well.

1¼ cups warm water [105 to 115 degrees]
2 packages dry yeast
5½-5 ¾ cups flour
1¼ cups mashed cooked winter squash
¼ cup molasses
2 tablespoons vegetable oil
1½ teaspoon salt
1 cup plus 2 tablespoons quick-cooking oats, uncooked and divided
 Vegetable cooking spray
1 tablespoon water

1. In large mixing bowl, combine yeast in warm water; let stand 5 minutes.

2. To the yeast mixture, add 2 cups flour, squash, molasses, vegetable oil and salt. Beat at medium speed of an electric mixer until smooth.

3. Stir in 1 cup oats and 2 more cups flour. Stir until well mixed.

4. Stir in 1 more cup flour.

5. Turn dough out onto lightly floured surface. Knead until smooth and elastic adding enough of the remaining flour, ¼ cup at a time to prevent dough from sticking to hands.

6. Place dough in large bowl coated with cooking spray, turning to coat top.

7. Cover with oiled plastic wrap and let rise in warm place until doubles in bulk.

8. Coat two 8x4 inch baking pans with cooking spray; sprinkle each with 1½ teaspoons oats.

9. Punch dough down and shape into loaves.

10. Put dough in prepared pans, seam side down.

11. Brush loaves with 1 tablespoon water and sprinkle with remaining 1 tablespoon oats.

12. Cover with oiled plastic wrap and let rise in warm place until doubled in bulk.

[continued]

OATMEAL SQUASH BREAD [continued]

13. Bake in preheated 350 degree oven 45-50 minutes or until loaves sound hollow when tapped.

14. Remove from pans immediately, and cool on wire racks.

SWISS STYLE FRENCH BREAD

[Serves 8-12]

It never ceases to amaze me how quickly slices of hot French bread disappear when passed around the dinner table. Add a splash of Swiss cheese and you'd better make two loaves so there are second and third trips around the hungry circle.

½   **cup margarine or butter, softened**
1   **tablespoon minced onion**
1   **tablespoon lemon juice**
1½ **teaspoons poppy seed**
1½ **teaspoons prepared mustard**
1   **cup shredded Swiss cheese**
1   **[16 ounce] loaf French bread**

1. In small mixing bowl, combine margarine, onion, lemon juice, poppy seed, mustard and Swiss cheese. Mix well.

2. Cut French bread into slices and spread with margarine mixture.

3. Wrap in foil and heat in preheated 350 degree oven for 20-30 minutes.

FLORENCE'S "DIFFERENT" CINNAMON ROLLS

[Makes 2 dozen rolls]

Yellow cake mix is the surprise ingredient in these feather light cinnamon rolls. The other unusual factor is that I've never met Florence Erdley of Caldwell, Idaho, who shared this recipe with me through the mail. When she wrote of the gorgeous easy to handle dough, I had to try it myself. I agree, this is an exceptional roll recipe.

2½ cups warm water [105-115 degrees]
2 packages quick rising yeast
1 [18.5 ounce] box yellow cake mix
1 cup flour
2 eggs
½ cup vegetable oil
1 teaspoon salt
5½ cups flour
4 tablespoons margarine or butter, softened, divided
½ cup sugar
1 tablespoon plus 1 teaspoon ground cinnamon

1. In large mixing bowl, dissolve yeast in warm water. Let stand a few minutes to begin activating the yeast.

2. Add cake mix, 1 cup flour, eggs, oil, and salt. Beat well.

3. Add remaining 5 ½ cups flour, beating with mixer as long as possible. When batter becomes stiff, stir with wooden spoon or use dough hook on mixer.

4. Put dough on floured surface and gently knead until smooth and elastic.

5. Put into oiled mixing bowl. Cover with oiled plastic wrap. Let dough double in bulk.

6. Punch down dough. Divide in half.

7. Roll one half into rectangle, 10x12 inches. Spread with 2 tablespoons of softened margarine.

8. Mix the sugar and cinnamon together. Spread half of this mixture over margarine.

[continued]

FLORENCE'S "DIFFERENT" CINNAMON ROLLS [continued]

9. Roll up, beginning at 12 inch side. Pinch edge firmly to seal. Stretch roll to make it an even 12 inches long.

10. Cut roll into twelve 1 inch slices. [I like to use an 8 inch length of string or thread to cut the slices. Just put the center of the string under the middle of the yeast bread you wish to slice. Pull the string in opposite directions to cut the slices]

11. Place the slices in greased 9x13 inch baking pan.

12. Cover with oiled plastic wrap.

13. Repeat procedure with other half of dough.

14. When doubled in bulk, remove plastic wrap. Bake in preheated 350 degree oven for 30-40 minutes until light golden brown. Remove from pan as soon as the rolls come out of the oven.

15. Drizzle with butter frosting, if you wish. Make frosting with 1½ cups confectioners' sugar, 2 tablespoons margarine, softened and 1 teaspoon vanilla. Add 1-2 tablespoons water, 1 tablespoon at a time, until desired consistency.

PARMESAN CHEESE LOAF

[Serves 8-10]

Hot French bread is a welcome addition to any quick menu. Add Parmesan cheese and you'll create a flavor to savor.

½   cup margarine or butter, softened
6   tablespoons grated Parmesan cheese
1   [16 ounce] loaf French or Vienna bread

1. In small mixing bowl, combine margarine and Parmesan cheese.

2. With serrated knife, slice bread into slices as thick or thin as desired.

3. Spread one side of each slice with margarine mixture.

4. Place spread slices on aluminum foil to reshape the loaf. Wrap tightly.

5. Bake in preheated 350 degree oven 15-20 minutes.

COUNTRY BROWN BREAD IN A BAG

[Makes l loaf]

Kids ages 6-80 think it's great fun to make a loaf of bread in a bag. Here is the step by step plan, written for bakers of all ages, to follow. Trust me, the directions aren't as complicated as they look. Share this idea with a friend soon.

1. In a two gallon heavy plastic bag put:

½   **cup flour**
1   **package active dry yeast**
½   **cup warm water [105-115 degrees]**
1   **tablespoon honey or sugar**

2. Squeeze upper part of bag to force out air. Close top of bag tightly between thumb and index finger.

3. Rest bag on table; mix by working bag with fingers about 20 seconds or until all ingredients are completely blended.

4. Prop bag up in 8x4 inch baking pan. Let mixture REST in bag 15 minutes.

5. Add these ingredients to the mixture in the bag:

¾   **cup warm water [105-115 degrees]**
1   **tablespoon honey or sugar**
2   **tablespoons nonfat dry milk powder**
1   **tablespoon vegetable oil**
1½ **teaspoons salt**

6. Mix by working outside of bag with fingers.

7. Add **2 cups whole wheat flour;** work outside of bag with fingers until flour disappears.

8. Gradually add **1¼ cups more flour** working mixture on outside of bag with fingers until stiff dough forms or until dough pulls away from bag.

9. Turn bread out onto floured surface.

10. Knead dough about 5 minutes or until dough is smooth and elastic. Add more flour, if necessary.

11. Cover dough with plastic bag. Let REST 10 minutes.

[continued]

COUNTRY BROWN BREAD IN A BAG

[continued]

12. Flatten dough into a 7x12 inch rectangle. At narrow end, fold corners to center to form a point. Beginning with point, roll dough tightly towards you. Pinch the edges to seal. Press dough at each end to seal and fold ends under.

13. Place seam side down in a well greased 8x4 inch loaf pan. Cover with oiled plastic wrap and let rise in warm place until doubled in bulk.

14. Bake on lower rack in preheated 400 degree oven 30-40 minutes or until deep golden brown. Remove from pan immediately. Cool.

HEART SMART HOT BREAD

[Serves 8]

Your heart healthy friends will send kudos your way if you reveal that butter-flavored vegetable cooking spray is used in this hot bread recipe. It's a great idea that works very well.

½ [1-pound] loaf Italian bread
  Butter-flavored vegetable cooking spray
¼ teaspoon garlic powder
2 tablespoons grated Parmesan cheese

1. Slice bread in half horizontally.

2. Spray each half with cooking spray.

3. In small bowl, combine garlic powder with Parmesan cheese.

4. Sprinkle bread halves with cheese garlic mixture.

5. Wrap in aluminum foil, and bake in preheated 350 degree oven for 20 minutes or until thoroughly heated.

MOLDED PEACH MELBA DELIGHT

[Serves 8]

When the menu calls for a lovely gelatin salad, this recipe would be an excellent suggestion. The sparkling peach and raspberry flavors are worthy of the extra few minutes it takes to create two separate layers.

1   [3 ounce] package raspberry flavored gelatin
1   cup boiling water
¾   cup cold water
1   cup fresh red raspberries or 1 [10 ounce] package frozen
    raspberries, thawed [use syrup as part of the cold water]
1   [3 ounce] package peach or apricot flavored gelatin
¾   cup boiling water
2   medium peaches, peeled & sliced [should make 1 cup puree]
2   tablespoons lemon juice
1   cup whipped topping or ½ cup heavy cream, whipped
    Lettuce leaves
    Peach slices for garnish, if desired

1. In medium bowl, dissolve raspberry gelatin in 1 cup boiling water. Stir in cold water.

2. Refrigerate until mixture is thickened, but not set.

3. Fold in raspberries.

4. Pour into oiled 6-cup mold.

5. Meanwhile, dissolve peach gelatin in 3/4 cup boiling water; cool.

6. In blender or food processor container, combine peaches and lemon juice; blend or process until smooth.

7. Add 1 cup of this peach mixture to peach gelatin.

8. Refrigerate until thickened, but not set.

9. Fold in whipped topping.

10. Pour mixture over raspberry gelatin. Refrigerate until firm.

11. To serve, unmold onto lettuce-lined plate. Garnish with additional fruit, if desired.

APRICOT NECTAR SALAD

[Serves 4-6]

One way to put pizzazz into a gelatin salad is to use fruit juice as part of the liquid. That's the function of apricot nectar in this delightful fruit bedecked offering.

1   [12 ounce] can apricot nectar [1 and ½ cups]
1   [3 ounce] package lemon flavored gelatin
⅓   cup water
1   tablespoon lemon juice
1   [11 ounce] can mandarin oranges, drained
1   cup halved seedless green grapes
1   medium red eating apple, cored, unpeeled, and chopped

1. In small saucepan, bring apricot nectar to a boil.

2. Pour hot nectar over gelatin. Stir to dissolve.

3. Stir in water and lemon juice.

4. Chill until consistency of unbeaten egg whites.

5. Stir in oranges, grapes and apple.

6. Pour into an oiled 4-cup mold or pretty serving dish.

7. Unmold or serve in dish. Garnish with greens and apple slices, if desired.

Microwave

In step 1, pour apricot nectar in 1 quart microwave-safe measurer. Microwave on 100% power 2-3 minutes, until boiling.

SUGAR-FREE APPLESAUCE SALAD

[Serves 4]

When a menu calls for a sugar-free gelatin salad, here is a great suggestion. The bright red color and smooth texture will bring smiles to the faces of family members and friends.

1½ cups unsweetened applesauce
1 tablespoon lemon juice
1 [0.3 ounce] package sugar-free cherry flavored gelatin
1 [8 ounce] can crushed pineapple in juice, undrained
¾ cup sugar-free lemon-lime carbonated beverage

1. Combine applesauce and lemon juice in a saucepan; bring to a boil.

2. Remove from heat; add gelatin, stirring until dissolved. Cool.

3. Add undrained pineapple and carbonated beverage; spoon into pretty serving dish or 4 cup oiled mold.

4. Chill until firm.

Microwave

In step 1, combine applesauce and lemon juice in 1 quart microwave-safe measurer. Microwave on 100% power for 3-5 minutes.

CRANAPPLE GELATIN SALAD

[Serves 4-6]

The minute I tasted this cranberry salad, I knew it was going to become one of my favorites. The apple juice gives a depth of flavor often desired in gelatin salads.

2 cups fresh or frozen cranberries, chopped
¾ cup sugar
1½ cups apple juice, divided
1 envelope unflavored gelatin
1 unpeeled apple, chopped
¼ cup chopped celery
¼ cup chopped pecans

1. Stir cranberries and sugar together in large bowl. Set aside.

2. In saucepan, sprinkle gelatin over ½ cup of the apple juice.

[continued]

CRANAPPLE GELATIN SALAD [continued]

3. Stir over low heat until gelatin dissolves.

4. Add remaining 1 cup apple juice.

5. Combine gelatin mixture with cranberries.

6. Stir in apples, celery and pecans.

7. Pour into pretty dish or 6 cup oiled salad mold.

8. Chill until firm.

Microwave

In step **2**, put ½ cup apple juice in 1 cup microwave-safe measurer. Let gelatin soften in juice a minute or two.

In step **3**, microwave on 100% power 30-45 seconds, until gelatin dissolves, stirring every 15 seconds.

APPLE CIDER SALAD

[Serves 8-10]

In autumn when apples are abundant and apple cider presses work overtime, this gelatin salad is a natural. Full of flavor and color, this salad is a glistening amber beauty.

3½ cups apple cider, divided
2   [3 ounce] packages orange-flavored gelatin
1   cup raisins
2   cups coarsely chopped, unpeeled apple
1   cup chopped celery
Grated rind and juice of 1 lemon
Lettuce leaves, if desired

1. Bring 2 cups apple cider to a boil; remove from heat.

2. Add gelatin and stir until dissolved.

3. Stir in raisins. Let cool.

4. Add remaining 1 and ½ cups apple cider; chill until consistency of unbeaten egg white.

5. Stir in apple, celery, lemon rind and juice.

6. Pour into a lightly oiled six cup mold or pretty serving dish.

7. Chill until set.

8. Unmold onto lettuce leaves, if desired

Fruit Fiesta

[Serves 6-8]

Lots of cooks constantly search for interesting recipes with short ingredient lists. Look no further for a fruit idea. Here is a winner. Change the fruits with the season and this salad is perfectly dressed for any occasion.

2   tablespoons sugar
1   tablespoon cornstarch
1   cup orange juice
6-8 cups assorted fresh or well-drained canned fruit which has been cut
     into bite-size pieces. Use pineapple, apples, oranges, bananas, kiwi,
     grapes, melon and/or peaches, etc.

1. Combine sugar and cornstarch in small saucepan. Stir in orange juice.

2. Cook and stir constantly over low heat until mixture thickens.

3. Chill.

4. Add chilled glaze to assorted fruits, gently stirring to cover fruit with glaze.

Microwave

In step 1, combine sugar and cornstarch in 1 quart microwave-safe measurer. Stir in orange juice.

In step 2, cook on full power 2-3 minutes, stirring every minute until thickened.

Yogurt Ambrosia

[Serves 6-8]

Traditionally, ambrosia is a mixture of fruit and coconut. This version is so versatile it could easily double as dessert.

1   [11 ounce] can mandarin oranges, drained
1   [20 ounce] can pineapple tidbits or chunks, drained
1½   cups seedless grapes
1   banana, peeled and sliced
1   cup miniature marshmallows
½   cup flaked coconut
¼   cup slivered almonds, toasted
1   [8 ounce] carton vanilla yogurt, [1 cup]

[continued]

YOGURT AMBROSIA [continued]

1. In large bowl, combine drained oranges and pineapple with grapes, banana, marshmallows, coconut and almonds.

2. Fold in yogurt.

3. Chill, if time permits.

4. Garnish and serve.

APPLE YUM YUM SALAD

[Serves 10-12]

Apples are teamed with pineapple and peanuts to create this appealing salad. It would be a great recipe to take along to a potluck supper. One word of warning, get ready for rave reviews.

1   **tablespoon flour**
½   **cup sugar**
1   **egg**
2   **tablespoons cider vinegar**
1   **[8 ounce] can crushed pineapple, drained, reserve juice**
4   **cups chopped crisp unpeeled apples**
1   **cup salted shelled peanuts**
1   **[8 ounce] carton nondairy frozen topping, thawed**

1. In small saucepan, combine flour and sugar; mix well.

2. Beat egg with fork and add to flour/sugar mixture.

3. Add vinegar and reserved pineapple juice.

4. Cook over low heat until thick, stirring constantly. Cool.

5. In large mixing bowl, combine apples, pineapple, and peanuts.

6. Pour cooled dressing over fruit. Toss to coat.

7. Fold in nondairy topping.

8. Put into pretty serving dish. Garnish with additional apple slices and peanuts.

Microwave

In step **1**, In 2 cup microwave-safe measurer, combine flour and sugar; mix well.

In step **4**, microwave on 100% power 1-2 minutes, stirring every 30 seconds, until thick.

Sweet Cherry Salad

[Serves 6]

Our family usually enjoys fresh sweet cherries as a snack or quick dessert. However, on a day when you can find a few minutes for pitting the cherries, this luscious fruit salad combination is worthy of consideration.

2   tablespoons vegetable oil
2   tablespoons honey
2   tablespoons frozen lemonade concentrate, thawed
2   cups fresh sweet cherries, cut in half & pitted
½   cup seedless green grapes, halved
½   cup chopped celery
½   cup broken walnuts
1   medium banana, sliced

1. In jar with tight fitting lid, combine oil, honey and lemonade concentrate. Shake well.

2. In medium mixing bowl, combine cherries, grapes, celery, walnuts and dressing. Gently mix together. Chill.

3. Just before serving, add sliced banana and toss lightly.

Strawberry Kiwi Salad

[Serves 4]

Ruby red strawberries and emerald green kiwis shine in this colorful salad. Just add the easy-to-create dill flavored dressing for a first-class experience.

¼   cup vegetable oil
¼   cup honey
¼   cup tarragon or cider vinegar
½   teaspoon dill weed
4   cups torn salad greens
1   pint strawberries, washed, hulled and sliced
2   kiwi fruit, peeled and sliced

1. In jar with tight fitting lid, combine oil, honey, vinegar and dill weed. Shake until well mixed. Chill to develop flavors, if time permits.

2. In salad bowl or on individual plates, place salad greens.

[continued]

STRAWBERRY KIWI SALAD [continued]

3. Arrange strawberries and kiwi on greens.

4. Just before serving, shake dressing and drizzle over salad ingredients. Toss together, if desired.

HOT FRUIT MEDLEY

[Serves 8-10]

Every once in a while it's fun to serve favorite foods in a new and different setting and/or temperature. Just look at the popular fruits all lined up in this recipe waiting to be heated and served for an interesting brunch or luncheon.

1   [16 ounce] can purple plums, drained
1   [16 ounce] can pears, quartered, drained
1   [16 ounce] can sliced peaches, drained
1   [20 ounce] can pineapple tidbits or chunks, drained
¼   cup margarine or butter, melted
½   cup brown sugar
1½ cups applesauce
½   cup maraschino cherries, drained
½   cup slivered or sliced almonds

1. Arrange drained plums, pears, peaches and pineapple in 2 quart ovenproof serving dish.

2. Blend together melted margarine and brown sugar.

3. Drizzle mixture over fruit.

4. Gently spread applesauce over fruit.

5. Top with maraschino cherries and almonds.

6. Bake, uncovered, in preheated 350 degree oven about 45 minutes or until piping hot.

HERBED APPLE SALAD

[Serves 4]

Marjoram, a member of the mint family, has a pleasing, spicy sweet flavor that beautifully enhances this simple apple salad. I think it would be a great addition to a roast pork menu.

2   **cups diced unpeeled apples**
½   **cup raisins**
1   **[8 ounce] can pineapple tidbits, drained**
¼   **cup light or regular mayonnaise or salad dressing**
1   **teaspoon dried marjoram leaves, crushed**
2   **tablespoons orange juice**

   1. Toss apples, raisins and pineapple together.

   2. Mix together mayonnaise, marjoram, and orange juice.

   3. Add mayonnaise mixture to fruit; toss lightly.

   4. Transfer to pretty serving dish.

   5. Garnish with extra apple slices, if desired.

ORANGE SALAD WITH HONEY DRESSING

[Serves 8]

It's such fun to make first class dressings using ingredients found in your kitchen. This excellent example is both pretty and palate pleasing when drizzled over oranges and greens.

⅓   **cup sugar**
2½   **tablespoons lemon juice**
2½   **tablespoons honey**
2   **tablespoons vinegar**
½   **teaspoon dry mustard**
½   **teaspoon paprika**
⅛   **teaspoon salt**
⅛   **teaspoon celery seeds**
½   **cup vegetable oil**
     Salad greens
5   **oranges, peeled and sliced**

[continued]

ORANGE SALAD WITH HONEY DRESSING [continued]

1. In container of blender or food processor, combine sugar, lemon juice, honey, vinegar, mustard, paprika, salt and celery seeds. Process until smooth.

2. While blender or food processor is running, slowly pour oil through the opening in the top; continue to process a few seconds until mixture is in suspension. Cover and chill.

3. At serving time, line individual salad plates with salad greens; arrange orange slices on greens and drizzle with dressing.

FRUIT AND PASTA SALAD

[Serves 6-8]

This recipe is a gentle reminder that pasta enhances fruit as well as vegetables. It's the perfect salad to take on a picnic to Lake Michigan.

1	**cup interesting pasta [i.e. shells or bowties]**
1	**[20 ounce] can pineapple tidbits or chunks, drained**
1	**[11 ounce] can mandarin orange segments, drained**
1	**cup halved seedless red or green grapes**
1	**large banana, sliced**
⅓	**cup shredded coconut**
1	**tablespoon frozen orange juice concentrate, thawed**
2	**tablespoons honey**
⅛	**teaspoon salt**
⅛	**teaspoon ground ginger**

1. Cook pasta to desired doneness as directed on package. Drain; rinse with cold water.

2. In large bowl, combine cooked pasta, pineapple, orange segments, grapes, banana and coconut.

3. In small bowl, combine orange juice concentrate, honey, salt and ginger.

4. Pour dressing over pasta mixture; toss lightly.

5. Refrigerate until chilled, before serving.

Pear and Grape Salad

[Serves 4]

It's fun to create mouth watering salads with popular ingredients. Here is an excellent example which uses the interesting combination of spinach and fruit.

¼   cup lemon juice
2   tablespoons vegetable oil
2   tablespoons honey
3   cups torn spinach leaves
1   medium pear, sliced
1   cup seedless red grapes
½   cup sliced celery
¼   cup pecan pieces

1. In jar with tight-fitting lid, combine lemon juice, oil, and honey; shake well.

2. Refrigerate to blend flavors.

3. At serving time, place spinach on large platter or individual salad plates.

4. Arrange pear, grapes, celery and pecans decoratively on top.

5. Drizzle with dressing.

FROZEN FRUIT CUPS

[Serves 12-16]

Here is one of my all time favorite frozen fruit ideas. Equally delicious when served as a salad, dessert, or snack, it's efficient to freeze this mixture in individual portions for quick and easy serving.

⅓ **cup sugar**
1 **[6 ounce] can frozen orange juice concentrate, [¾ cup]**
1 **[6 ounce] can frozen pink lemonade concentrate, [¾ cup]**
1 **[10 ounce] package frozen sliced strawberries, thawed**
1 **[10 ounce] package frozen raspberries, thawed**
1 **[20 ounce] can unsweetened crushed pineapple, undrained**
1 **[12 ounce] can sugar free or regular ginger ale [1½ cups]**

1. In large mixing bowl, combine sugar, orange juice concentrate, pink lemonade concentrate, strawberries, raspberries and crushed pineapple. Stir until sugar dissolves.

2. Add ginger ale; stir gently. Pour into 5 ounce paper cups or other non-metal container. Freeze firm.

3. Store in freezer in airtight container.

CANTALOUPE 'N GREENS

[Serves 6-8]

It's easy to be so interested in selecting a variety of vegetables for tossed salads that we forget all of the fruit possibilities. For a change of pace, do try this cantaloupe and greens combination, complete with homemade dressing.

DRESSING:

½	cup sugar
½	teaspoon salt
1	teaspoon dry mustard
1	teaspoon paprika
½	teaspoon celery seed
⅓	cup vinegar
¾	cup vegetable oil
1	tablespoon grated onion

6	cups torn salad greens
1½	cups cantaloupe cubes or balls
½	cup toasted sliced almonds
	Generous sprinkle of celery seeds
1	kiwi fruit, peeled and sliced

1. In saucepan, combine sugar, salt, dry mustard, paprika, ½ teaspoon celery seed, and vinegar. Bring to a boil, stirring until sugar dissolves.

2. Cool.

3. In jar with tight fitting lid, combine cooled mixture with oil and onion. Cover tightly. Shake well.

4. Store dressing in refrigerator up to 1 month.

5. At serving time, layer greens, cantaloupe and almonds in salad bowl. Sprinkle with celery seeds.

6. Add some dressing and toss very gently.

7. Top with kiwi fruit slices.

Microwave

In step **1**, combine sugar, salt, dry mustard, paprika, ½ teaspoon celery seed and vinegar in 2 cup microwave-safe measurer. Microwave on 100% power 30-60 seconds, stirring once, until sugar dissolves.

ROMAINE/ORANGE SALAD

[Serves 8]

Romaine is a trusted salad green you'll find readily available at most produce counters. It's the perfect base for this delicious dressing and delicate mandarin oranges.

½   **cup vegetable oil**
2   **tablespoons vinegar**
2   **tablespoons lemon juice**
2   **tablespoons honey**
¼   **teaspoon salt**
1   **teaspoon Dijon mustard**
1   **pound romaine lettuce, washed, dried, and torn**
½   **cup sliced green onions**
1   **[11 ounce] can mandarin oranges, chilled and drained**
¼   **cup sunflower seeds**

1. In jar with tight fitting lid, combine oil, vinegar, lemon juice, honey, salt and mustard. Shake very well. Chill, if time permits.

2. In pretty salad bowl, combine romaine, green onions, and mandarin oranges.

3. Just before serving, drizzle dressing over greens and toss to coat.

4. Garnish with sunflower seeds.

LIGHT AND LOVELY TOSSED SALAD

[Serves 8]

In just a matter of minutes, it's easy to put together this delicious salad dressing. Remember that by measuring the honey in the same spoon that was used for the oil, the honey releases with spectacular speed.

4	tablespoons olive or vegetable oil [¼ cup]
2	tablespoons honey
2	tablespoons white wine or herb vinegar
⅛	teaspoon garlic powder
⅛	teaspoon salt
⅛	teaspoon dry mustard
¼	teaspoon ground pepper
12	cups washed, dried, and torn salad greens
2	cups shredded carrots
1	tomato, cut into wedges

1. In small jar with tight-fitting lid, combine oil, honey, vinegar, garlic powder, salt, mustard and pepper. Shake well. Chill to blend flavors, if time permits.

2. Place greens and carrots in salad bowl or large plastic bag.

3. Just before serving, pour dressing over greens; toss lightly.

4. Garnish with tomato wedges.

VIBRANT VEGETABLE SALAD

[Serves 6]

Red cabbage is often featured in restaurant garden salads but forgotten by the everyday cook. This pretty salad remembers the vibrant color of red cabbage as well as carrots and radishes. The quick fat free dressing tastefully coats the crunchy vegetables.

DRESSING:

3	tablespoons white wine or flavored vinegar
¼	cup sugar
¼	teaspoon salt
¼	teaspoon celery seed

[continued]

VIBRANT VEGETABLE SALAD [continued]

4   **cups torn crisp salad greens**
1   **cup shredded red cabbage**
1   **cup sliced carrots**
½   **cup sliced fresh mushrooms**
½   **cup sliced radishes**

1. In jar with tight fitting lid, combine vinegar, sugar, salt and celery seed. Shake well to combine.

2. In salad bowl, combine salad greens, cabbage, carrots, mushrooms and radishes.

3. Just before serving, shake dressing and pour over salad.

4. Toss to coat vegetables evenly with dressing.

GREEK STYLE SALAD

[Serves 8-10]

Every once in a while I like to serve feta cheese in a tossed green salad. Here is a vegetable combination and dressing that are worthy of such a wonderful pungent cheese.

6   **cups torn romaine lettuce leaves**
6   **cups torn leaf lettuce leaves**
8   **cherry tomatoes, halved**
1   **large unpeeled cucumber, sliced**
1   **[16 ounce] can pitted black olives, drained**
½   **cup olive oil**
3   **tablespoons red wine vinegar**
1   **teaspoon dried whole oregano leaves, crushed**
¼   **teaspoon ground pepper**
1   **cup crumbled feta cheese**

1. Combine romaine and leaf lettuce leaves, cherry tomatoes, cucumber and olives in large salad bowl. Toss gently.

2. Combine olive oil, vinegar, oregano, and pepper in jar;cover tightly, and shake vigorously.

3. Just before serving, toss salad with dressing. Sprinkle with f

ROMAINE SALAD DELUXE

[Serves 10-12]

If the occasion calls for a green salad extraordinaire, this classy combination is the perfect selection. You will usually find canned hearts of palm near the canned artichoke hearts at the grocery store.

1   [14 ounce] can artichoke hearts, drained and quartered
1   [14 ounce] can hearts of palm, drained and sliced
1   medium onion, thinly sliced and separated into rings
½   cup white wine vinegar
¼   cup water
1   tablespoon olive oil
¼   teaspoon ground pepper
¼   teaspoon oregano leaves, crushed
⅛   teaspoon garlic powder
1   [10 ounce] head romaine salad greens, washed, dried & torn
8   cherry tomatoes, halved
2   tablespoons grated Parmesan cheese

1. Combine artichokes, hearts of palm and onion in a shallow dish.

2. Combine vinegar, water, oil, pepper, oregano, and garlic powder in a glass jar. Cover tightly and shake vigorously.

3. Pour over vegetable mixture, tossing well.

4. Cover and refrigerate 8 hours or overnight, toss occasionally.

5. Drain vegetable mixture, reserving marinade.

6. Combine romaine and marinated vegetables in a large salad bowl; toss gently.

7. Arrange cherry tomatoes on top of salad. Sprinkle salad with Parmesan cheese.

8. Serve with reserved marinade as salad dressing.

ASPARAGUS AND STRAWBERRY VINAIGRETTE

[Serves 4]

When spring comes to Michigan, it's easy to get caught up in the world of homegrown asparagus and strawberries. This easy to create salad is a classy way to show off these two favorite produce items.

¼   **cup lemon juice**
1   **tablespoon vegetable oil**
1   **tablespoon honey**
    Pinch of ground ginger
½   **pound fresh asparagus**
    Fresh garden greens
2   **cups sliced fresh strawberries**

1. In small jar with tight fitting lid, combine lemon juice, oil, honey, and ginger. Shake well to combine. Chill.

2. Cut asparagus into 1½ inch pieces.

3. Cook in small amount of water until crisp tender.

4. Drain. Plunge into cold water to stop cooking process. Drain again. Chill until serving time.

5. Line salad plates with garden greens.

6. Arrange asparagus and strawberries on greens.

7. Drizzle with lemon mixture.

Microwave

In step **3**, cook asparagus with 1 tablespoon water in 1 quart covered microwave-safe container for 3-4 minutes on full power, stirring once until crisp tender.

Pea Salad

[Serves 6-8]

Here is a great salad idea for family meals and casual entertaining that comes from my sister-in-law, Martha House, who lives near Seattle, Washington. You may be surprised to know that emerald green peas are as delicious cold as they are hot.

1   (16 ounce) bag frozen petite peas, thawed
6   green onions, thinly sliced
1   (8 ounce) can sliced water chestnuts, drained
4   slices bacon, fried and crumbled
¼   cup light or regular sour cream
¼   cup light or regular mayonnaise
½   teaspoon dill weed
    Salt and freshly ground pepper to taste
    Grated cheddar cheese for garnish, if desired

1. In mixing bowl, combine thawed peas, green onions, water chestnuts and bacon.

2. In small bowl, whisk together sour cream, mayonnaise and dill weed.

3. Add dressing to pea mixture. Mix well.

4. Season with salt and pepper as desired.

5. Chill to develop flavors.

6. At serving time, garnish with cheddar cheese, if desired.

Marinated Zucchini

[Serves 6]

The next time you're looking for ways to use zucchini, remember this flavorful salad idea. The marinade enhances fresh zucchini in a first class way. Lots of times, I use a resealable plastic bag for the marinating process.

3   medium zucchini, thinly sliced [6 cups]
⅓   cup cider vinegar
¼   cup sweet pickle relish
2   tablespoons chopped onion

[continued]

Marinated Zucchini [continued]

3   tablespoons vegetable oil
1   [2-ounce] jar diced pimiento, drained
½   teaspoon salt
⅛   teaspoon pepper
⅛   teaspoon garlic powder

1. Place sliced zucchini in bowl or resealable plastic bag.

2. Combine vinegar, pickle relish, onion, oil, pimiento, salt, pepper and garlic powder.

3. Pour mixture over zucchini; toss to coat zucchini.

4. Cover and chill at least 8 hours to develop flavor.

Colorful Marinated Asparagus Salad

[Serves 6]

This mixture could easily win a five star award when it comes to eye appeal. Add to that winning status full bodied flavor, this idea is destined to become part of your permanent recipe file.

2   cups cut-up fresh asparagus
8   cherry tomatoes, halved
½   cup diced yellow bell pepper
¼   cup sliced ripe olives
½   cup prepared Italian salad dressing

1. Cook asparagus in rapidly boiling water for 3-5 minutes or until crisp tender; drain. Rinse with cold water until asparagus is cold.

2. In self-sealing plastic bag or non-metal bowl, combine asparagus, tomatoes, pepper, ripe olives and dressing.

3. Toss gently to coat vegetables evenly with dressing.

4. Seal bag or cover; refrigerate 1-2 hours to blend flavors.

Microwave

In step 1, place asparagus in 2-quart microwave-safe dish; add ¼ cup water. Cover with lid or vented plastic wrap. Microwave on 100% power 3-6 minutes or until crisp tender, stirring once during cooking; drain. Rinse with cold water until asparagus is cold.

TABBOULEH

[Serves 10-12]

A salad of Lebanese origin, tabbouleh characteristically contains bulgur and a variety of garden produce. Bulgur is wheat that has been cooked and dried, then cracked. It can be found at the grocery store near health foods or with other cereals. Bulgur is also a popular bulk food item.

2	cups bulgur
2	cups boiling water
2	cups chopped tomatoes
½	cup finely sliced green onions
1½	cups finely chopped parsley
¼	cup finely chopped mint
½	cup extra virgin olive oil or vegetable oil
½	cup lemon juice
1	teaspoon salt
¼	teaspoon garlic powder

1. In large bowl, pour boiling water over bulgur. Let stand 1 hour. Drain, if any water is not absorbed.

2. Add tomatoes, green onions, parsley and mint; mix well.

3. In 1 cup glass measurer, combine oil, lemon juice, salt and garlic powder. Whisk together to evenly combine.

4. Add dressing to bulgur mixture. Stir thoroughly.

5. Chill until serving time.

Note:

I like to chop the parsley and mint in a food processor. Remember that tabbouleh stores very well in the refrigerator. It's a great salad to brighten light meals.

TURNIP AND CARROT SLAW

[Serves 6-8]

If you're part of the group that prefers raw carrots over cooked carrots, it's very possible that you'll like the crisp fresh texture and taste of raw turnips too. Just try this savory slaw and find out.

4	**cups grated turnips**
2	**cups grated carrots**
½	**cup chopped red onion**
¾	**cup sugar**
1	**cup cider vinegar**
½	**cup oil**
1	**teaspoon celery seed**
1	**teaspoon dry mustard**
½	**teaspoon salt**

1. In mixing bowl, toss together turnips, carrots and onion.

2. In medium saucepan, combine sugar, vinegar, oil, celery seed, dry mustard and salt.

3. Over medium heat, bring mixture to a boil, stirring occasionally.

4. Pour dressing over vegetables.

5. Chill thoroughly to develop flavors.

Microwave

In step **2**, in 2 quart microwave-safe measurer, combine sugar, vinegar, oil, celery seed, dry mustard and salt.

In step **3**, microwave mixture on 100% power 4-6 minutes, stirring twice, until mixture boils.

MICHIGAN GARDEN RELISH

[Serves 6-8]

When it's harvest time here in Michigan, good cooks create lots of ways to serve the bounties of this good earth. Here is a plan that features a light dressing that's lightning quick to fix.

3   tomatoes, coarsely chopped
1   cucumber, peeled, seeded, and sliced
1   green pepper, diced
1   small onion, sliced and separated into rings
1   tablespoon sugar
2   tablespoons water
1   tablespoon vinegar
½   teaspoon salt
¼   teaspoon celery seed
¼   teaspoon ground pepper

1. In mixing bowl, combine tomatoes, cucumber, green pepper and onion rings.

2. In small saucepan, combine sugar, water, vinegar, salt, celery seed and pepper.

3. Heat just until sugar and salt are dissolved.

4. Pour liquid mixture over vegetables.

5. Cover and chill well before serving.

Microwave

In step **2**, combine sugar, water, vinegar, salt, celery seed and pepper in 1 cup microwave-safe measurer.

In step **3**, microwave on 100% power 30-45 seconds, stirring once to dissolve sugar and salt.

OLD FASHIONED COLESLAW

[Serves 6]

For many of us who grew up on farms here in the Midwest, cabbage slaw was a hearty standby in the world of salads. Some variations had a mayonnaise type dressing while others, like this recipe, had a delicately seasoned sugar vinegar mixture coating the vegetables.

¼   cup sugar
2   tablespoons white vinegar
2   tablespoons water
¼   teaspoon celery seed
⅛   teaspoon salt
⅛   teaspoon mustard seed
3   cups shredded cabbage
⅓   cup chopped celery
⅓   cup chopped green pepper
2   tablespoons chopped red pepper or pimiento

1. In small saucepan, combine sugar, vinegar, water, celery seed, salt and mustard seed.

2. Bring to a boil, stirring constantly to dissolve sugar. Cool.

3. Combine cabbage, celery, green pepper and red pepper.

4. Pour cooled dressing over vegetables; toss to coat.

5. Cover; refrigerate several hours to blend flavors.

Microwave

In step **1**, in 2-cup microwave-safe measurer, combine sugar, vinegar, water, celery seed, salt and mustard seed.

In step **2**, microwave on 100% power 45-60 seconds. Stir. Cool.

ZESTY CAULIFLOWER SALAD

[Serves 8]

If your taste buds favor cauliflower, then do try this palate pleasing salad recipe. A few simple ingredients serve as both the marinade and the dressing.

1   small head cauliflower, cut into bite-size pieces
½   cup vegetable oil
2   tablespoons white wine or herb flavored vinegar
1   tablespoon lemon juice
1   teaspoon dry mustard
½   teaspoon garlic salt
¼   teaspoon tarragon leaves
     Dash pepper
½   cup sliced ripe olives
¼   cup sliced green onions
8   cups assorted salad greens, washed, dried, and torn

1. In saucepan, cook cauliflower in boiling water until crisp-tender; drain. Chill by rinsing in cold water.

2. In medium bowl, combine oil, vinegar, lemon juice, mustard, garlic salt, tarragon and pepper; whisk well.

3. Add cooked cauliflower, olives and green onions; toss gently. Refrigerate until well chilled.

4. Just before serving, combine cauliflower mixture with salad greens in large salad bowl; toss gently. Serve immediately.

Microwave

In step **1**, cook cauliflower in 2-quart microwave-safe casserole with small amount of water, covered, for 6-8 minutes on 100% power. Drain. Chill by rinsing in cold water.

ASPARAGUS WITH TOASTED PECANS

[Serves 3-4]

On a busy day when you're in need of a quick asparagus garnish, try this pleasing pecan idea. As with most toppings, the recipe doubles or triples easily.

1 **pound fresh asparagus, spears or cut into short lengths**
¼ **cup water**
¼ **teaspoon salt**
2 **tablespoons margarine or butter**
2 **tablespoons chopped pecans**

1. Cook asparagus in boiling salted water until crisp tender. Drain well.

2. Melt margarine in small skillet; add pecans.

3. Cook and stir pecans until they are toasted.

4. Garnish cooked asparagus with toasted pecans.

Microwave

In step **1**, cook asparagus in covered 2 quart microwave-safe casserole, 5-7 minutes on 100% power, stirring once, until asparagus is crisp tender.

In step **2**, microwave margarine 15-30 seconds on 100% power in small microwave-safe dish; add pecans.

In step **3**, microwave on 100% power for 1-2 minutes, stirring every 30 seconds until pecans are toasted.

CRANBERRY GLAZED BEETS

[Serves 6]

There's no doubt about it. These ruby red glazed beets will add optimum color along with great flavor to any menu.

1 **tablespoon cornstarch**
1 **tablespoon sugar**
  Dash of salt
1 **cup cranberry juice cocktail**
2 **[16 ounce] cans diced or sliced beets, drained**

1. In medium saucepan, stir together cornstarch, sugar and dash of salt.

2. Gradually stir in cranberry juice.

3. Cook and stir over medium heat until mixture thickens and bubbles.

4. Add beets to sauce.

5. Simmer, uncovered, 10 minutes or until piping hot.

Microwave

In step **1**, stir together cornstarch, sugar and dash of salt in 2 quart microwave-safe measurer or casserole.

In step **3**, microwave on 100% power 2-3 minutes, stirring every minute, until thickened.

In step **5**, microwave on 100% power 4-6 minutes, stirring once or twice.

BROCCOLI POLONAISE

[Serves 4]

"Polonaise" means to top with crumbs and is traditionally used on vegetables like broccoli. It's an almost "instant" way to turn a rather ordinary vegetable into a special offering.

1 **pound fresh broccoli or 1 [16 oz.] package frozen broccoli cuts**
½ **cup water**
¼ **cup margarine or butter**
½ **cup dry bread crumbs**
1 **tablespoon grated Parmesan cheese**
1 **hard cooked egg, finely chopped, if desired**

1. Clean fresh broccoli and cut into bite size pieces.

2. In medium saucepan, bring water to a boil. Add broccoli; return to a boil.

3. Stir; reduce heat. Cover; simmer 6 to 8 minutes or until crisp-tender. Drain.

4. Meanwhile, melt margarine in small saucepan over medium-high heat. Add bread crumbs and Parmesan cheese; stir until bread crumbs are golden brown.

5. Place broccoli in serving bowl. Add bread crumb mixture; toss gently.

6. Sprinkle with chopped egg, if desired.

Microwave

In step **2**, combine broccoli and ¼ cup water in 2 quart microwave-safe casserole. Cover with lid or vented plastic wrap.

In step **3**, microwave on 100% power 6-8 minutes or until crisp-tender, stirring once halfway through cooking. Drain. Place in serving bowl; cover and keep warm.

In step **4**, put margarine in 2 cup microwave-safe measuring cup. Microwave on 100% power 30-45 seconds or until melted. Stir in bread crumbs and Parmesan cheese. Microwave on 100% power 1-3 minutes or until bread crumbs are golden brown, stirring twice during cooking.

Brussels Sprouts En Casserole

[Serves 6-8]

Lots of cooks keep an eagle eye out for easy creative ways to serve vegetables. Look no further for a delicious recipe to showcase Brussels sprouts. Here is a palate pleasing plan.

2 **[10 ounce] packages frozen Brussels sprouts**
2 **eggs**
1½ **cups soft bread crumbs [2 slices]**
1 **[10 and ¾ ounce] can cream of mushroom soup**
½ **cup shredded Cheddar cheese [2 ounces]**
2 **tablespoons chopped onion**
   Dash of pepper
2 **tablespoons margarine or butter, melted**

1. Cook Brussels sprouts according to package directions; drain. Cut sprouts into fourths and set aside.

2. In medium mixing bowl, beat eggs slightly with a fork. Add ¾ cup of the crumbs, soup, cheese, onion and pepper, Mix well.

3. Fold in Brussels sprouts.

4. Transfer mixture to lightly greased 1 and ½ quart casserole.

5. Combine remaining crumbs and melted margarine; sprinkle on top of the sprouts.

6. Bake, uncovered, in a preheated 350 degree oven for 30-40 minutes or until hot and bubbly.

Microwave

In step **1**, combine Brussels sprouts and onion in 1½ quart microwave-safe casserole. Microwave on 100% power 10-12 minutes, stirring once. Drain. Cut sprouts into fourths and set aside.

In step **4**, return mixture to same casserole.

In step **5**, do not put crumb/margarine mixture on top of sprouts until casserole is hot.

In step **6** microwave, uncovered, on 100% power 8-10 minutes, stirring once, until mixture is hot and bubbly. Sprinkle with reserved crumbs. Microwave on 100% power 1-2 minutes longer.

CAULIFLOWER/BROCCOLI PARMESAN

[Serves 6]

Here is an easy, creamy, cheesy sauce that adds real class to broccoli and cauliflower. Even folks who say they never eat vegetables will like this recipe.

2   cups fresh cauliflower flowerets
2   cups fresh broccoli flowerets
1   tablespoon margarine or butter
1   [3 ounce] package cream cheese, softened
3   tablespoons grated Parmesan cheese
¼   cup milk
1   teaspoon dried parsley flakes
¼   teaspoon paprika

1. In medium saucepan, cook cauliflower and broccoli in small amount of boiling water until crisp tender. Drain. Keep warm.

2. In small saucepan, combine margarine, cream cheese, Parmesan cheese and milk. Heat over low heat, stirring constantly until smooth and hot.

3. Put vegetables in serving dish.

4. Top with hot sauce.

5. Sprinkle with parsley and paprika.

Microwave

In step **1**, put cauliflower and broccoli in 2 quart microwave-safe casserole. Add ¼ cup water. Microwave on 100% power 6-8 minutes, until vegetables are crisp tender, stirring once. Drain. Keep warm.

In step **2**, put margarine in 2 cup microwave-safe measurer. Microwave on 100% power 15-30 seconds. Add cream cheese, Parmesan cheese and milk. Microwave on 50% power 2-3 minutes or until smooth and thoroughly heated, stirring once.

GLAZED BABY CARROTS

[Serves 4]

In recent years, baby carrots have grown in popularity because they are conveniently ready to use. Add just a few ingredients and you'll produce a lovely hot vegetable for family and friends.

1   [16 ounce] package baby carrots
2   tablespoons margarine or butter
3   tablespoons brown sugar
2   tablespoons orange juice
½   teaspoon ground ginger
    Chopped fresh or dried parsley

1. In saucepan, cook carrots in small amount of boiling water until crisp tender; drain.

2. In small saucepan, melt margarine; add brown sugar, orange juice and ginger. Heat until bubbly.

3. Pour mixture over carrots and toss gently.

4. Garnish with chopped parsley.

Microwave

In step 1, put carrots in 1 quart microwave-safe casserole. Add 2 tablespoons water. Cover with lid or vented plastic wrap. Microwave on 100% power 6-8 minutes, until crisp tender, stirring once. Drain.

In step 2, put margarine in 2 cup microwave-safe measurer. Microwave on 100% power 15-30 seconds to melt; add brown sugar, orange juice and ginger. Microwave on 100% power 30-45 seconds, stirring once.

EGGPLANT PARMESAN

[Serves 4-6]

Eggplant is a favorite summer vegetable of my Minnesota sister-in-law, Betsey House, so I'm grateful she shared this well-tested recipe. Although not all family members share her eggplant enthusiasm, over the years she has managed to "educate" her husband, Ross House, so that he now even allows it in the garden.

1	**large eggplant**
3	**eggs, beaten**
1	**cup dried bread crumbs**
	Olive oil for frying
½	**cup grated Parmesan cheese**
1	**teaspoon oregano leaves, crushed**
1	**teaspoon basil leaves, crushed**
½	**pound Mozzarella cheese, sliced**
3	**[8 ounce] cans tomato sauce**

1. Pare eggplant and cut into ¼ inch slices.

2. Dip each slice into eggs, then into crumbs.

3. Heat oil in shallow skillet.

4. Saute eggplant slices in hot oil until golden brown on both sides.

5. Place layer of eggplant in 2 quart casserole; sprinkle with some of the Parmesan cheese, oregano and basil.

6. Top with some of the Mozzarella slices and cover with part of the sauce.

7. Repeat layers until all eggplant is used.

8. Top with several slices of Mozzarella cheese.

9. Bake, uncovered, in preheated 350 degree oven 30-40 minutes or until sauce is bubbly and cheese is melted.

GREEN BEANS WITH CHERRY TOMATOES

[Serves 6-8]

Whenever I see bushels of fresh green beans at outdoor markets or roadside stands, this colorful vegetable recipe comes to mind. If fresh basil leaves are available, they provide a wonderful pungent flavor, however remember dried basil could be used too.

1½ **pounds fresh green beans**
1½ **cups water**
¼ **cup margarine or butter**
1 **tablespoon sugar**
¾ **teaspoon garlic salt**
⅛ **teaspoon salt**
¼ **teaspoon pepper**
1½ **teaspoon chopped fresh basil or ½ teaspoon dried**
   basil leaves, crushed
2 **cups halved cherry tomatoes**

1. Wash beans; trim ends and remove strings. Cut into 1½ inch pieces.

2. Combine beans and water in a saucepan; bring to a boil. Cover, reduce heat and simmer about 15 minutes until crisp tender. Drain.

3. Melt margarine in skillet; stir in sugar, garlic salt, salt, pepper and basil. Add tomatoes; stir gently, cooking just until tender.

4. Pour tomatoes and sauce over beans; toss gently.

5. Transfer vegetables to pretty serving dish.

Microwave

In step **2**, combine beans with ½ cup water in 2 quart microwave-safe covered casserole. Microwave on 100% power 9-11 minutes, stirring once, until crisp tender. Drain.

In step **3**, melt margarine in 1 quart microwave-safe casserole in microwave on 100% power for 30 seconds. Stir in sugar, garlic salt, salt, pepper, and basil. Add tomatoes; stir gently. Microwave on 100% power 2-4 minutes, stirring every minute until tomatoes are tender.

CHEESY BAKED CORN

[Serves 10-12]

One reason vegetable casseroles are popular with menu planners is that they often can be prepared ahead of time, refrigerated and baked when needed. Such is the case in this yummy corn casserole.

2   tablespoons margarine or butter
4   teaspoons flour
⅛   teaspoon garlic powder
¾   cup milk
1½ cups shredded sharp cheddar cheese
1   [3 ounce] package cream cheese, cut up
2   [16 ounce] packages frozen whole kernel corn, thawed
1   cup diced or chopped ham
     Paprika

1. In large saucepan, melt margarine. Stir in flour and garlic powder. Add milk all at once.

2. Cook and stir over medium heat until thickened and bubbly.

3. Stir in cheddar and cream cheese. Cook and stir until cheese melts.

4. Add corn and ham. Mix thoroughly.

5. Transfer mixture to lightly greased 2 quart casserole. Sprinkle with paprika.

6. Cover and refrigerate up to 24 hours, if desired.

7. Bake in preheated 350 degree oven 45-50 minutes or until hot and bubbly.

Microwave

In step **1**, put margarine in 3 quart microwave-safe casserole. Microwave on 100% power 20-30 seconds until margarine melts. Stir in flour and garlic powder. Add milk.

In step **2**, microwave on 100% power 2-4 minutes, stirring every minute with whisk, until thickened.

In step **3**, add Cheddar and cream cheese. Microwave on 100% power 1-2 minutes until cheese melts, stirring once.

In step **5**, use 2 quart microwave-safe casserole.

In step **7**, use microwave probe set to 160 degrees at 80% power.

FAVORITE CORN CASSEROLE

[Serves 8]

Ever since several students in a Portage Community Education class shared this recipe with me, it has been a favored vegetable idea for family gatherings. The ingredient list is so short and simple that soon you'll have it memorized.

2   **eggs**
1   **[16 ounce] can whole kernel corn, drained**
1   **[16 ounce] can cream style corn**
½ **cup margarine or butter, melted**
1   **[8 and ½ ounce] package corn muffin mix**
1   **cup light or regular sour cream**

1. In mixing bowl, beat eggs with fork.

2. Add drained corn, cream style corn, melted margarine, muffin mix and sour cream. Stir thoroughly to combine.

3. Bake in preheated 350 degree oven 45-55 minutes or until center is set.

4. Garnish with fresh parsley.

GRILLED MARINATED VEGETABLES

[Serves 6]

This marinade is flavored with fresh marjoram, a tender perennial herb from the mint family. Remember that grilltop screens or racks help keep small pieces of food, such as cut-up vegetables, from falling onto the coals. It's the perfect way to cook summertime vegetables.

3   **small zucchini, cut lengthwise in half**
3   **small yellow squash, cut lengthwise in half**
1   **red or green bell pepper, cut into 6 pieces**
1   **large sweet onion, cut into ½ inch slices**
⅓ **cup olive oil or vegetable oil**
1   **tablespoon lemon juice**
2   **teaspoons, finely chopped fresh marjoram or ½ teaspoon dried marjoram leaves**
¼ **teaspoon salt**
⅛ **teaspoon garlic powder**
⅛ **teaspoon pepper**

[continued]

GRILLED MARINATED VEGETABLES [continued]

1. Arrange vegetables in a 2 quart flat baking dish.

2. Combine oil, lemon juice, marjoram, salt, garlic powder and pepper. Mix well.

3. Pour marinade over vegetables. Cover and let stand at least 1 hour.

4. Remove vegetables from marinade and place on grilltop screen; reserve marinade.

5. Cover and grill vegetables over medium coals 10-15 minutes, turning and brushing 2 or 3 times with marinade, until golden brown and tender.

POTATO FANS

[Serves 6]

This potato idea captures the best of two worlds....the moist tenderness of a baked potato and the crisp crustiness of a french fried potato. By putting each potato in a large spoon for the slicing procedure, the knife is prevented from cutting through the entire potato, thus fans are able to spread apart during baking.

6   **medium to large baking potatoes**
2   **tablespoons margarine or butter, melted**
    Salt, pepper, and paprika as desired
2   **tablespoons grated Parmesan cheese**

1. Peel potatoes and place in cold water.

2. To make potato fan, place potato in large spoon. Using sharp knife and without cutting completely through potato, slice potato crosswise into ⅛ inch slices.

3. Return to cold water. Repeat with remaining potatoes.

4. Drain potatoes; place in foil lined and lightly greased 8 inch square pan.

5. Brush the potatoes with half the margarine.

6. Bake in preheated 400 degree oven for 40 minutes.

7. Brush with remaining margarine and sprinkle with salt, pepper and paprika as desired.

8. Sprinkle with Parmesan cheese.

9. Bake an additional 20-25 minutes or until potatoes are tender and lightly browned.

Do-Ahead Mashed Potatoes

[Serves 12]

One of the most often used recipes in my first cookbook, *House Specialties*, is the make ahead mashed potato idea. Here is an updated version that is considerably lower in fat and sodium than the original version.

5	**pounds potatoes, peeled & quartered**
6	**ounces Neufchatel light cream cheese**
1	**cup light sour cream**
2	**egg whites**
2	**teaspoons onion powder**
1	**teaspoon salt**
¼	**teaspoon white pepper**
1	**tablespoon margarine**

1. Cook potatoes in boiling water until tender; drain.

2. Mash until smooth. [I like to put the potatoes through a potato ricer and then use an electric mixer. This assures no lumps.]

3. Add Neufchatel cheese, sour cream, egg whites, onion powder, salt and pepper. Beat until light and fluffy. Cool.

4. Cover and place in refrigerator. These may be used any time within two weeks.

5. To use, place desired amount in greased casserole, dot with margarine and bake in preheated 350 degree oven until heated through, 30-40 minutes. The entire recipe fills a two-quart casserole.

Microwave

In step **5**, put potatoes in microwave-safe casserole and probe to 150 degrees using 80% power.

Pecan-Orange Sweet Potatoes

[Serves 8-10]

This recipe reminds me of family gatherings complete with holiday meals, however these flavors would be welcome any time of the year. Efficient cooks will appreciate the make ahead factor of this festive sweet potato casserole.

8   medium sized sweet potatoes, cooked
2   oranges, peeled and thinly sliced
2½   tablespoons cornstarch
1   cup brown sugar
½   teaspoon salt
2   tablespoons grated orange rind
¼   cup margarine or butter
2   cups orange juice
½   cup pecan halves

1. Peel and slice potatoes into 1 inch slices.

2. Arrange alternate layers of sweet potatoes and orange slices in 2 quart lightly greased casserole.

3. In saucepan, combine cornstarch, brown sugar and salt; add orange rind and margarine. Pour in orange juice and cook over low heat, stirring constantly, until smooth and thickened.

4. Pour sauce over sweet potatoes and oranges. Top with pecans.

5. If desired, cover and refrigerate up to 24 hours.

6. Bake, uncovered, in preheated 350 degree oven about 30-40 minutes or until hot and bubbly.

Microwave

In step **3**, combine cornstarch, brown sugar and salt in 2 quart microwave-safe measurer. Add orange rind and margarine. Stir in orange juice. Microwave on 100% power 4-7 minutes, until thickened, stirring every minute or two.

CRANBERRY-FILLED ACORN SQUASH

[Serves 4]

Acorn squash halves are one of nature's natural bowls, so it's up to creative cooks to fill the hollowed out indentations. For color and flavor, the cranberries that are suggested in this recipe are a first class choice.

2	medium acorn squash
3	cups fresh or frozen cranberries
¾	cup apple juice, divided
¾	cup sugar
¼	teaspoon ground cloves
¼	teaspoon ground nutmeg
2	teaspoons cornstarch
1	tablespoon chopped walnuts

1. Cut squash in half; remove seed and fibers.

2. Bake squash, cut side down, in flat pan in preheated 350 degree oven about 1 hour, until tender.

3. In medium saucepan, combine cranberries, ½ cup apple juice, sugar, cloves and nutmeg. Cook over low heat until cranberry skins pop.

4. Combine remaining ¼ cup apple juice with cornstarch, mixing well. Gradually stir into cranberry mixture, mixing well.

5. Heat and stir just until thickened.

6. Spoon cranberry mixture into squash shells.

7. Sprinkle cranberries with chopped walnuts.

8. Place in a preheated oven for 10 minutes or until piping hot.

Microwave

In step **2**, cover each squash half with plastic wrap and arrange about one inch apart in microwave oven. Microwave on 100% power 12-18 minutes or until soft to the touch, rearranging squash half way through cooking time.

In step **3**, in 2 quart microwave-safe measurer, combine cranberries, ½ cup apple juice, sugar, cloves and nutmeg. Microwave on 100% power 8-12 minutes, stirring once or twice until cranberry skins pop.

In step **5**, microwave on 100% power 2-3 minutes until mixture thickens, stirring once or twice.

In step **8**, microwave on 80% power 3-5 minutes until piping hot.

SQUASH AMANDINE

[Serves 8]

This great winter squash recipe comes from the treasured recipe file of my friend, Alice Leach. Any variety of winter squash works well, however my favorites are buttercup or butternut.

¼ cup margarine or butter, melted
2 eggs
4 cups cooked winter squash, mashed, or 2 [10 ounce] packages frozen winter squash, thawed
¼ cup brown sugar
¼ cup light or regular sour cream
1 teaspoon salt
⅛ teaspoon ground nutmeg
½ cup sliced almonds, divided

1. In large mixing bowl, beat together melted margarine and eggs with beater.
2. Stir in squash, brown sugar, sour cream, salt and nutmeg. Thoroughly combine ingredients.
3. Reserve 2 tablespoons sliced almonds. Chop remaining almonds and add to squash mixture. Stir well.
4. Transfer squash to lightly greased 1 ½ quart casserole.
5. Top with reserved 2 tablespoons of sliced almonds.
6. Bake in preheated 350 degree oven 30-40 minutes or until lightly browned and piping hot.

Microwave

[Refer to *More House Specialties* cookbook page 222 for microwave directions for cooking winter squash.]

In step **4**, use microwave-safe casserole.

In step **6**, microwave, uncovered, at 80% power until hot. [Length of time will depend on starting temperature of squash] Or probe squash to 150 degrees at 80% power of the microwave.

SCALLOPED SLICED TOMATOES

[Serves 6-8]

On a day when a few tomatoes wait to be used, pull this recipe from your repertoire. Plain down home ingredients turn themselves into a classy vegetable casserole.

4   **medium tomatoes, unpeeled or peeled**
¼   **cup margarine or butter**
½   **cup chopped onion**
1   **cup diced celery**
½   **teaspoon salt**
1   **teaspoon sugar**
1   **teaspoon basil leaves, crumbled**
⅛   **teaspoon ground pepper**
1   **cup plain croutons**

1. Cut tomatoes into ¼-½ inch slices.

2. Overlap tomatoes in two rows in lightly greased 8x12 inch casserole; set aside.

3. In medium saucepan, melt margarine. Add onions and celery; saute until vegetables are tender.

4. Stir in salt, sugar, basil and pepper.

5. Spoon all but ¼ cup celery mixture over the tomatoes.

6. Toss croutons with reserved ¼ cup celery mixture and spoon down center of casserole between the tomatoes.

7. Cover with foil and bake in preheated 350 degree oven 30 minutes or until tomatoes are cooked.

Microwave

In step **2**, use microwave-safe 2 quart dish.

In step **3**, put margarine in 1 quart microwave-safe casserole. Microwave on 100% 30 seconds. Add onions and celery. Microwave on 100% power 3-4 minutes, stirring once, until vegetables are tender.

In step **7**, cover with vented plastic wrap. Microwave on 80% power 12-15 minutes, rotating dish halfway through cooking time, or until tomatoes are cooked.

FIRST CLASS VEGETABLE CASSEROLE

[Serves 8-10]

Here is a winning vegetable casserole combination that can be made ahead and enjoyed at home or toted to the next pot luck gathering. It could also win an award for ease of preparation.

1   [10 and ¾ ounce] can cream of mushroom soup, undiluted
1   [8 ounce] jar processed cheese spread
1   [5 ounce] can evaporated milk [⅔ cup]
¼   teaspoon garlic powder
1   [16 ounce] can whole green beans, drained
2   [14 ounce] cans artichoke hearts, drained and quartered
1   [8 ounce] can sliced mushrooms, drained
1   [16 ounce] package frozen broccoli cuts
¾   cup sliced green onions
2   tablespoons margarine or butter, melted
1½ cups soft bread crumbs [2 slices]

1. In saucepan, combine soup, cheese spread, evaporated milk and garlic powder.

2. Cook over medium heat until mixture is smooth, stirring often.

3. In large mixing bowl, combine green beans, artichoke hearts, mushrooms, broccoli and green onion.

4. Spoon half of vegetable mixture into a lightly greased 8x12 inch casserole; pour half of the sauce over vegetables.

5. Repeat procedure with remaining vegetables and sauce.

6. Combine melted margarine with bread crumbs; sprinkle over casserole.

7. Cover casserole and refrigerate up to 8 hours, if desired.

8. Uncover. Bake in preheated 350 degree oven for 40-45 minutes or until bubbly and lightly browned.

Microwave

In step **1**, in 2 quart microwave-safe measurer, combine soup, cheese spread, evaporated milk and garlic powder.

In step **2**, microwave on 100% power 2-4 minutes, stirring every minute until mixture is smooth.

MINI PUMPKIN SURPRISE

[One per person]

For years, I thought miniature pumpkins were non-edible gourds. But then I followed baking instructions and found out they tasted just like winter squash. They are both attractive and delicious.

1 **miniature pumpkin per person**
Brown sugar and margarine as desired
Sprinkle of cinnamon and nutmeg

1. Cut off the very top of each pumpkin...about a quarter of the way down.

2. Scoop out the seeds and strings.

3. Put desired amount of brown sugar and margarine in each pumpkin. Sprinkle with cinnamon and nutmeg, if desired.

4. Put top back on pumpkin.

5. Place pumpkins on cookie sheet.

6. Bake in preheated 350 degree oven 45-55 minutes or until fork tender.

Microwave

In step **6**, microwave each pumpkin on 100% power 4-6 minutes, rotating once, until fork tender.

SQUASH RED PEPPER STIR-FRY

[Serves 4-6]

Tender zucchini and yellow summer squash are perfect candidates for the stir-fry method of cooking. Add a splash of color with vibrant red pepper strips and you'll have an eye appealing quick-to-fix vegetable.

3 **cups thinly sliced zucchini or yellow summer squash**
½ **medium red bell pepper, cut into 2 and ½ inch strips**
1 **small onion, thinly sliced, separated into rings**
2 **teaspoons vegetable oil**
¼ **teaspoon salt**
¼ **teaspoon marjoram leaves, crushed**
⅛ **teaspoon pepper**

[continued]

Squash Red Pepper Stir-Fry [continued]

1. In large bowl, combine squash, pepper and onion.

2. Heat large skillet over medium-high heat until hot.

3. Add oil; heat until it ripples.

4. Add vegetables; stir-fry 5-6 minutes or until crisp-tender.

5. Season with salt, marjoram and pepper.

Zucchini and Tomato Bake

[Serves 4-6]

Baked vegetables are a great help to the busy cook because they eliminate last minute hassles that can happen just before serving time. This zucchini and tomato combination proves the point.

Vegetable cooking spray
3½ cups sliced zucchini
1   cup sliced onion
1   green pepper, halved, seeded and cut into strips
½   teaspoon dried Italian seasoning
¼   teaspoon garlic powder
¼   teaspoon ground pepper
1   [16 ounce] can tomatoes, undrained and chopped

1. Spray 1½ quart casserole with vegetable spray.

2. Layer zucchini, sliced onion and green pepper strips in casserole.

3. In small dish, combine Italian seasoning, garlic powder and pepper. Sprinkle seasonings over vegetable layers.

4. Pour tomatoes over casserole.

5. Bake uncovered in preheated 350 degree oven for about 1 hour.

Microwave

In step **1**, use microwave-safe 1½ quart casserole.

In step **5**, microwave on 100% power 10 minutes, rotating dish once. Continue to microwave on 80% power 10-15 minutes more until zucchini is tender, rotating dish once.

SPEEDY "REFRIED" BEANS

[Serves 4]

Health and fitness fans have reawakened the entire world to the benefits of bean cuisine. Protein-packed and high in soluble fiber, beans are low in fat and calories. Keep the pantry shelves well stocked and you can have these tasty beans in a hurry.

1 [15 ounce] can pinto or black beans, drained and rinsed
¼ cup picante or salsa sauce, mild, medium or hot
½ teaspoon ground cumin
½ teaspoon salt, if desired
½ cup grated lowfat or regular Cheddar cheese

1. In mixing bowl, put drained beans. Break up beans with a potato masher.

2. Add picante or salsa, cumin and salt.

3. Using low speed on an electric mixer, beat until mixture is fairly smooth.

4. Heat in saucepan over medium heat until hot.

5. Put into serving dish and top with cheese.

Microwave

In step **4**, put mixture in 2-cup microwave-safe dish. Microwave at 80% power for 5-7 minutes, rotating dish once.

In step **5**, after adding cheese, microwave on 80% power 1-2 minutes until cheese melts.

BEANS 'N RICE OLE

[Serves 6]

This wholesome combination of beans and rice is a great side dish idea or in another setting could actually serve as an entree. Cumin, an herb related to parsley and a close cousin to caraway, adds an interesting warm depth to the mild flavor of rice and beans. Of course, cumin teams beautifully with picante or salsa sauce.

2½ **cups water**
2　**teaspoons instant chicken bouillon, if desired**
1　**teaspoon ground cumin**
1　**cup converted long grain rice**
1　**[16 ounce] can black, pinto or kidney beans, drained and rinsed**
¾　**cup picante or salsa sauce, mild, medium or hot**

1. In medium saucepan, bring water and bouillon to a boil.

2. Add cumin and rice. Return to a boil, stirring several times.

3. Cover. Reduce heat to simmer.

4. Cook 22-25 minutes, until water is absorbed.

5. Remove from heat.

6. Stir drained beans and picante sauce into cooked rice.

7. Return to burner and heat just until piping hot.

Microwave

In step **1**, in 3 quart microwave-safe casserole, put water and bouillon. Microwave on 100% power, covered, 5 minutes or until boiling.

In step **2**, add cumin and rice. Microwave on 100% power, covered, for 3-4 minutes. Stir.

In step **4**, microwave on 50% power, covered, for 12-14 minutes, stirring once or twice. Allow 5 minutes standing time.

In step **7**, microwave on 80% power, covered, for 3-5 minutes until piping hot.

Note: If chicken bouillon is not used, add salt to taste.

CURRIED BROWN RICE

[Serves 6]

Brown rice gets great reviews for its high fiber qualities. For added flavor, this interesting recipe includes a hint of curry and tiny bits of dried apricot.

Vegetable cooking spray
½ **cup sliced green onion**
2½ **cups water**
2 **teaspoons instant chicken bouillon**
¼ **cup snipped dried apricots**
½ -1 **teaspoon curry powder**
1 **cup uncooked brown rice**
2 **tablespoons chopped fresh parsley**

1. Coat a medium saucepan with cooking spray. Place over medium heat until hot; add onion and saute until tender.

2. Add water, bouillon, apricots and curry.

3. Bring water mixture to a boil.

4. Add rice. Cover, reduce heat, and simmer 50 minutes or until liquid is absorbed.

5. Stir in chopped parsley.

6. Serve.

GARDEN RICE PILAF

[Serves 4]

If you're planning a menu that includes rice, this vegetable studded pilaf is an interesting recipe. It takes about the same length of time to cook rice in the conventional or microwave oven, however the microwave oven takes honors for reheating rice. Just remember to use 80% power to insure even reheating.

2½ **cups water**
1 **tablespoon instant chicken bouillon**
1 **cup converted long grain rice**
1 **cup frozen loose packed mixed vegetables or peas**

[continued]

GARDEN RICE PILAF [continued]

1. Bring water and chicken bouillon to a boil.

2. Stir in rice; return to boiling. Cover; reduce heat and simmer 15 minutes.

3. Stir in frozen vegetables and continue to cook 5-8 minutes until all moisture is absorbed.

CELEBRATION RICE

[Serves 12]

When family members and friends gather together, it's the perfect time to bring out this group size recipe. Celebrate a birthday, holiday or just the fact that everyone is together.

¼   **cup margarine or butter**
1   **cup sliced green onions**
1   **cup shredded carrots**
2½ **cups uncooked converted long grain rice**
5   **teaspoons instant chicken bouillon**
¼   **teaspoon dried thyme leaves**
4½ **cups water**
½   **cup chopped fresh parsley**

1. Melt margarine in 4-quart Dutch oven.

2. Saute green onions and carrots in melted margarine.

3. Add rice; cook, stirring occasionally, until rice is opaque.

4. Add bouillon, thyme, and water.

5. Cook over high heat until mixture comes to a boil.

6. Cover. Reduce heat and simmer 15-20 minutes or until liquid is absorbed.

7. Stir in parsley.

8. Serve to family and friends.

HEART SMART FETTUCCINE ALFREDO

[Serves 6]

Evaporated skim milk is the secret heart smart ingredient in this wonderful fettuccine. It's an outstanding side dish that you'll want to serve often.

8-9 ounces uncooked fettuccine
1 tablespoon margarine
¼ teaspoon garlic powder
1 cup evaporated skim milk
1 teaspoon instant chicken bouillon
3 tablespoons grated Parmesan cheese
1 teaspoon dried basil leaves
⅛ teaspoon nutmeg
¼ cup chopped fresh parsley

1. Cook fettuccine to desired doneness as directed on package. Drain, return to pan.

2. Add margarine and garlic; toss to coat.

3. Stir in evaporated milk, chicken bouillon, Parmesan cheese, basil and nutmeg; blend well.

4. Cook over medium-high heat just until thickened, about 5 minutes, stirring constantly.

5. Put in serving dish. Sprinkle with parsley.

6. Serve immediately.

4

Finale

Some folks may think that the significant recipes most treasured are found in this finale chapter.

Here you'll find recipes for comfort foods like angel food cake, bread pudding and cherry pie that bring to mind warm childhood memories. Included too, is a collection of creative cookie ideas that patiently wait to be baked.

To assist the health conscious cook, there is a thoughtful selection of delicious heartsmart desserts.

Contents

CHOCOLATE ANGEL FOOD CAKE

[Serves 10-12]

If the thought of making an angel food cake from scratch seems too overwhelming, think again....it's just a few simple ingredients put together in a very special way. The result is a light delicate chocolate cake that's the perfect finale for any heart healthy menu.

¾ **cup sifted cake flour**
¼ **cup unsweetened cocoa**
¾ **cup sugar**
1½ **cups egg whites**
1½ **teaspoons cream of tartar**
¼ **teaspoon salt**
1½ **teaspoons vanilla**
¾ **cup sugar**

1. Sift cake flour, cocoa and ¾ cup sugar together 4 times. Set aside.
2. Beat egg whites with cream of tartar, salt and vanilla until stiff enough to form soft peaks but are still moist and glossy.
3. Add the remaining ¾ cup sugar, 2 tablespoons at a time, continuing to beat until meringue holds stiff peaks.
4. Sift ¼ of flour mixture over whites; fold in.
5. Fold in remaining flour by fourths.
6. Push batter into ungreased 10 inch tube pan. Gently cut through batter with table knife.
7. Bake in preheated 375 degree oven for 35-40 minutes or until top springs back when touched lightly with finger.
8. Invert tube pan on funnel; let hang until cake is completely cool.

Mary's Marble Cupcakes

[Makes 18]

When my sister-in-law, Mary Howell of Dallas, Texas, wants to treat her family and friends to a home baked dessert, this is her favorite recipe. I'm quite certain your family and friends would put these cupcakes in the winning category too.

1½ cups flour
¼   cup unsweetened cocoa
1   cup sugar
1   teaspoon baking soda
½   teaspoon salt
1   cup water
½   cup vegetable oil
1   teaspoon vinegar
1   teaspoon vanilla
1   [8 ounce] package light or regular cream cheese, softened
1   egg
⅓   cup sugar
⅛   teaspoon salt
1   [6 ounce] package semisweet chocolate chips [1 cup]

1. In large mixing bowl, sift together flour, cocoa, 1 cup sugar, baking soda and 1/2 teaspoon salt. Make a well in middle of dry ingredients.

2. In well, pour water, oil, vinegar and vanilla.

3. Beat mixture until smooth. Set aside.

4. In medium mixing bowl, combine cream cheese, egg, 1/3 cup sugar and 1/8 teaspoon salt. Beat until mixture is smooth. Stir in chocolate chips.

5. Fill well greased or paper lined muffin cups about half full with chocolate batter.

6. Add 1 tablespoon cream cheese mixture on top of each batter-filled cupcake.

7. Bake in preheated 350 degree oven for about 20 minutes or until batter appears baked.

Chocolate Cake Roll

[Serves 8]

Tucked away in my file of recipes from special friends, I found this chocolate lovers cake roll idea. It came from Jo Miller, one of our treasured neighbors back home on the Howell family farm in southern Wisconsin. She often fills it with whipped cream and fresh or well drained fruit. Equally delicious is the frozen version filled with ice cream or frozen yogurt.

½ cup sifted cake flour
½ teaspoon baking powder
¼ teaspoon salt
4 eggs
¾ cup sifted granulated sugar
1 teaspoon vanilla
2 [1 ounce] squares unsweetened chocolate
2 tablespoons granulated sugar
¼ teaspoon baking soda
3 tablespoons cold water
   Fillings:
1 cup whipping cream, whipped, with favorite fruit
   or
1 quart ice cream or frozen yogurt, softened

1. Sift flour, baking powder and salt together 3 times.

2. Place eggs in a deep bowl, then gradually add ¾ cup sugar, while beating with an electric beater until very thick and lemon-colored.

3. Then add flour mixture, all at once, stirring until well mixed.

4. Add vanilla.

5. Melt chocolate in the microwave oven or over boiling water.

6. Remove from heat, and add immediately 2 tablespoons sugar, the soda and cold water. Stir until thick and light, then fold quickly into batter. Blend well.

7. Grease a 10½ x 15½ inch jelly roll pan and cover with parchment paper, waxed paper or foil [shiny side up]. Grease and lightly flour the paper or foil.

8. Spread batter evenly in pan and bake in preheated 375 degree oven about 15 minutes or until toothpick comes out clean.

[continued]

CHOCOLATE CAKE ROLL [continued]

9. While the cake is baking, liberally dust a kitchen towel with confectioners' sugar.

10. Turn cake out onto the towel, carefully remove paper or foil and trim off any crisp edges.

11. Roll the cake up in the towel from the long side and let it rest 1 minute. Unroll and let cake rest for a few minutes, then roll up in towel again and cool completely.

12. Unroll and spread with whipped cream filling or softened ice cream or frozen yogurt.

13. Roll up without the towel.

14. Sprinkle with confectioners' sugar or frost with chocolate frosting, if desired.

15. Store in the refrigerator or freezer.

PINEAPPLE PUMPKIN CAKE

[Serves 18-20]

Totable cakes are popular fare at pot luck gatherings. Maybe that's why the 9x13 inch covered cake pan was invented. This pleasing pineapple pumpkin cake fits the pan and carries well.

2	cups flour
1	teaspoon baking powder
1	teaspoon baking soda
2	teaspoons ground cinnamon
½	teaspoon salt
1½	cups vegetable oil
2	cups sugar
4	eggs
1	teaspoon vanilla
1	cup cooked pumpkin
1	[8 ounce] can crushed pineapple, drained
	Confectioners' sugar, for topping

1. Sift together flour, baking powder, baking soda, cinnamon and salt. Set aside.

2. In large mixing bowl, beat together oil and sugar until well blended, using medium speed on electric mixer.

3. Add eggs, one at a time, beating well after each addition. Beat in vanilla and pumpkin.

4. Add dry ingredients; beat well.

5. Stir in pineapple.

6. Pour batter into greased and floured 9x13 inch baking pan.

7. Bake in preheated 350 degree oven 30-40 minutes or until cake tests done with wooden pick. Cool on rack.

8. Sprinkle with confectioners' sugar.

LOVELY LIGHT ORANGE POUND CAKE

[Makes 1 loaf]

The delicate flavor and beautiful texture of this cake remind me of the simple pleasures of life. These everyday ingredients are transformed into a cake worthy of accolades.

4   **egg whites**
1¾ **cups sifted cake flour**
2   **teaspoons baking powder**
¼   **teaspoon salt**
¾   **cup sugar**
½   **cup vegetable oil**
½   **cup unsweetened orange juice**
1   **teaspoon grated orange rind**

1. Beat egg whites until stiff. Set aside.

2. Sift together cake flour, baking powder, salt and sugar in large bowl.

3. Add oil and orange juice; with unwashed beaters of an electric mixer, beat at medium speed until well blended.

4. Add orange rind and about one-third of the egg white mixture; stir gently.

5. Fold in the remaining egg whites.

6. Pour batter in vegetable sprayed and parchment lined or floured 8x4 inch loaf pan.

7. Bake in preheated 350 degree oven for 45-55 minutes or until wooden pick inserted in center comes out clean.

8. Cool in pan 10 minutes; remove and cool on rack.

APPLE DESSERT

[Serves 10-12]

Fond memories surround this apple dessert because Gladys House would serve it to us during our visits back home in southern Wisconsin. Quite often, she used apples that she and Grandpa House had picked from their own trees.

4   cups diced tart peeled apples
2   cups sugar
2   cups flour
1½   teaspoons baking soda
1   teaspoon salt
2   teaspoons cinnamon
2   eggs, well beaten
¾   cup vegetable oil
2   teaspoons vanilla
1   cup chopped walnuts or pecans

1. In large mixing bowl, combine apples and sugar. Let stand for a few minutes.

2. Sift together flour, baking soda, salt and cinnamon.

3. Mix dry ingredients with apples.

4. In medium mixing bowl, combine beaten eggs with oil and vanilla. Stir in walnuts or pecans.

5. Add egg mixture to apples. Stir to evenly combine.

6. Pour mixture into a lightly greased 9x13 inch baking pan.

7. Bake in preheated 350 degree oven for 40-50 minutes.

8. Serve with whipped cream, if desired.

SOFT GINGERBREAD

[Serves 16-20]

Gingerbread is one of my "comfort" foods because it reminds me of country baking back on the family farm in southern Wisconsin. However, I would have to admit that this recipe, which comes from the Shaker tradition, is the best gingerbread I've ever tasted.

1	**cup boiling water**
1	**teaspoon baking soda**
½	**cup margarine or butter, softened**
1	**cup sugar**
1	**cup molasses**
2	**eggs**
2½	**cups flour**
1	**teaspoon ground ginger**
1	**teaspoon ground cinnamon**
1	**teaspoon ground nutmeg**
½	**teaspoon salt**

1. Dissolve soda in boiling water. Set aside.

2. Cream softened margarine or butter with electric mixer.

3. Add sugar a little at a time, creaming well after each addition.

4. Add molasses slowly and continue beating until mixture is light and creamy.

5. Add eggs, one at a time, to the creamed mixture, beating well after each addition.

6. Sift together the flour, ginger, cinnamon, nutmeg and salt.

7. Divide the combined flour and spices into four parts. Add one part at a time to the creamed mixture alternately with the cooled water-soda mixture, starting and ending with flour. Stir well with wooden spoon, but do not beat.

8. Pour batter into greased and floured 9x9 inch cake pan.

9. Drop the filled pan, a few times, lightly on the work surface to remove any air pockets that might produce tunneling.

10. Spread the batter to the edges of the pans so it is thicker at the edge that at the center. This will result in an even cake.

11. Bake in preheated 350 degree oven for about 45 minutes or until wooden pick comes out clean.

12. This gingerbread is lovely served with the Lemon Sauce on page 187.

BREAD PUDDING

[Serves 6-8]

My files have never contained a recipe for bread pudding. So you can imagine how appreciative I was to receive this outstanding recipe from my friend, Carolyn Mowbray of Janesville, Wisconsin. I like to serve the Lemon Sauce on page 187 with this scrumptious bread pudding.

2   **cups milk**
4   **eggs**
½   **cup sugar**
6   **tablespoons unsalted butter, melted**
1   **teaspoon ground cinnamon**
1   **teaspoon ground nutmeg**
6-7 **ounces of baguette, French bread or Vienna bread,**
     cut into 1 inch bread cubes [about 8 cups]
½   **cup pecan pieces**
¾   **cup raisins**

1. In large mixing bowl, whisk together milk, eggs, sugar, melted butter, cinnamon and nutmeg until sugar dissolves.

2. Add bread and set aside, stirring occasionally, until bread is completely soft, about 30 minutes.

3. Stir pecan pieces and raisins into the softened bread and pour into a lightly greased 1 and 1/2 quart baking dish.

4. Cover baking dish with foil or lid.

5. Place filled baking dish in a large pan of warm water. Water should be about halfway up the sides of the baking dish.

6. Bake in preheated 350 degree oven 30 minutes.

7. Remove foil and continue baking about 20 minutes or until center of bread pudding is set.

8. Serve with Lovely Lemon Sauce page 187. Omit nutmeg in Lemon Sauce recipe, if desired.

Lovely Lemon Sauce

[Makes 1½ cups]

The hint of nutmeg in this wonderful lemon sauce imparts an in-depth flavor worthy of your consideration. It's as delicious on fresh gingerbread as it is on bread pudding.

½ **cup sugar**
1   **tablespoon cornstarch**
1   **cup boiling water**
2   **tablespoons margarine or butter**
1½ **tablespoons lemon juice**
½ **teaspoon ground nutmeg**
¼ **teaspoon salt**

1. Mix sugar and cornstarch in saucepan; gradually add boiling water, stirring constantly. Cook and stir until thickened and mixture is well blended.

2. Remove from heat; add margarine, lemon juice, nutmeg, and salt.

3. Heat to blend flavors and serve warm over gingerbread, or bread pudding.

Microwave

In step **1**, mix sugar and cornstarch in 1 quart microwave-safe measurer. Add boiling water, stirring with whisk. Microwave on 100% power 1-2 minutes, until mixture thickens, stirring every minute.

In step **3**, microwave on 100% power about 1 minute to blend flavors.

Sunflower Crispies

[Makes 3 dozen]

As the popularity of sunflower seeds grows, interesting recipes like these crispy cookies are developed. They literally melt in your mouth, requiring most folks to enjoy at least two or three.

½   **cup margarine or butter, softened**
½   **cup sugar**
½   **cup brown sugar**
⅓   **cup vegetable oil**
1   **egg**
2   **cups flour**
½   **teaspoon cream of tartar**
½   **teaspoon baking soda**
½   **cup roasted, salted sunflower kernels**

1. In medium mixing bowl, beat together margarine, sugar, brown sugar and oil until smooth and creamy.

2. Add egg and beat well for 2-3 minutes.

3. Sift together flour, cream of tartar, and baking soda. Stir into creamed mixture.

4. Stir in sunflower kernels.

5. Drop dough onto parchment lined or ungreased cookie sheet with teaspoon or ejector spoon.

6. Bake in preheated 375 degree oven 10-12 minutes.

SPANISH PEANUT DROP COOKIES

[Makes 3-4 dozen]

One day when I was perusing recipes, I found this simple drop cookie idea. Since I had an ample supply of red skinned Spanish peanuts, it was my next baking project. The result is a crunchy cookie that will require keeping the pantry stocked with peanuts.

¾ **cup margarine or butter, softened**
1 **cup brown sugar**
¼ **cup creamy peanut butter**
1 **teaspoon vanilla**
1 **egg**
1¾ **cups flour**
1 **teaspoon baking soda**
¼ **teaspoon salt**
1 **cup Spanish peanuts**

1. In large mixing bowl, beat margarine, brown sugar and peanut butter until light and fluffy.

2. Add vanilla and egg; blend well.

3. Sift together flour, soda and salt.

4. Add to creamed mixture, stirring until flour disappears.

5. Stir in peanuts.

6. Drop by ejector spoon or heaping teaspoonfuls onto parchment lined or ungreased cookie sheet.

7. Bake in preheated 375 degree oven 8-12 minutes or until light golden brown.

8. Cool 1 minute; remove from cookie sheet.

ORANGE DELIGHTS

[Makes 5 dozen]

The light delicate orange flavor in this drop cookie is truly delightful. If you have trouble shredding orange peel, try putting the orange in the freezer for about 30 minutes before shredding the peel.

6   tablespoons margarine or butter, softened
⅓   cup vegetable shortening
1   cup sugar
2   eggs
⅔   cup buttermilk
2   teaspoons shredded orange peel
¼   cup orange juice
2⅔ cups flour
1   teaspoon baking powder
½   teaspoon baking soda
¼   teaspoon salt
     Orange Frosting [See recipe below]

1. In mixing bowl, cream together margarine, shortening and sugar.

2. Add eggs one at a time, beating well after each addition.

3. Beat in buttermilk, peel, and orange juice.

4. Sift together flour, baking powder, baking soda and salt.

5. Add dry ingredients to creamed mixture. Mix well.

6. Drop dough by ejector spoon or teaspoonfuls onto parchment lined or ungreased cookie sheet.

7. Bake in preheated 350 degree oven 10-12 minutes, until cookies are baked but not browned.

8. Cool on racks.

9. Frost with Orange Frosting, if desired.

ORANGE FROSTING:

3   cups sifted confectioners' sugar
1   tablespoon shredded orange peel
3-4 tablespoons orange juice

1. Beat together: to make a spreadable, thick frosting.

PAUL'S CHOCOLATE DROP COOKIES

[Makes 3 dozen cookies]

Our son, Paul, has enjoyed cookie baking since his early days in a 4-H Foods project. So it's not surprising that after a day in the chemistry lab he often bakes these favorite chocolate cookies.

½   cup margarine or butter, softened
1   cup brown sugar
1   teaspoon vanilla
2   [1 ounce] squares unsweetened chocolate, melted and cooled
1   egg
2   cups flour
½   teaspoon baking soda
½   teaspoon salt
¾   cup sour cream
½   cup chopped walnuts

1. In mixing bowl, cream together margarine and brown sugar until light and fluffy.

2. Beat vanilla, melted chocolate and egg into creamed mixture.

3. Sift together flour, soda, and salt.

4. Alternately add dry ingredients and sour cream to chocolate mixture, beginning and ending with flour. Mix well after each addition.

5. Stir in walnuts.

6. Drop by teaspoon or ejector spoon on lightly greased or parchment lined cookie sheet.

7. Bake in preheated 350 degree oven 10-14 minutes or until set.

8. Cool a minute or two; remove from cookie sheets.

9. Cool completely.

PEANUT BUTTER COOKIES

[Makes 3-4 dozen cookies]

When my friend, Rita Henquinet of Mason, Michigan, shared a canister of these family pleasing cookies with us they disappeared in double quick time. Maybe that's because these peanut butter cookies could easily be in the "comfort food" category.

1 **cup vegetable shortening**
1 **cup peanut butter**
1 **cup sugar**
1 **cup brown sugar**
2 **eggs**
2½ **cups flour**
1½ **teaspoons baking soda**
1 **teaspoon baking powder**
½ **teaspoon salt, if desired**

1. In medium mixing bowl, cream together shortening, peanut butter, sugar and brown sugar.

2. Add eggs, one at a time, beating well after each addition.

3. Add in flour, soda, baking powder and salt. Stir until all dry ingredients disappear.

4. Cover and chill.

5. Shape into 1-2 inch balls. Place on parchment lined or lightly greased cookie sheet.

6. With fork dipped in milk, flatten in crisscross pattern.

7. Bake in preheated 375 degree oven 10-12 minutes or until set, but not hard.

MARBLE BROWNIES

[Makes 4-5 dozen]

When my friend, Anne Reuther, from Milwaukee, shared this wonderful recipe with me she earmarked it a "Reuther Family Favorite". Both she and I hope that soon this efficient scrumptious recipe will be a favorite with your family too.

½   cup margarine
¾   cup water
2   [1 ounce] squares unsweetened chocolate
2   cups flour
2   cups sugar
1   teaspoon baking soda
½   teaspoon salt
2   eggs, well beaten
½   cup sour cream
1   [8 ounce] package cream cheese, softened
⅓   cup sugar
1   egg
1   [6 ounce] package mini chocolate chips [1 cup]

1. In a medium saucepan, combine margarine, water and chocolate.

2. Bring to a boil. Remove from heat.

3. Stir in flour, 2 cups sugar, baking soda and salt.

4. Add beaten eggs and sour cream; mix well.

5. Pour into greased and floured 10x15 inch jelly roll pan.

6. Spread batter evenly in pan.

7. In mixing bowl, beat together cream cheese, ⅓ cup sugar, and egg until smooth.

8. Gently dribble and spread cream cheese mixture over chocolate batter.

9. Cut through batter with knife several times for marble effect.

10. Sprinkle with chocolate chips.

11. Bake in preheated 375 degree oven for 30 minutes or until toothpick comes out clean.

12. Cool. Cut into squares.

ORANGE DATE BARS

[Makes 3-4 dozen]

The highlight of these mouth watering bar cookies, is an orange accented date filling sandwiched between two layers of brown sugar crust. They literally melt in your mouth.

1½ cups chopped pitted dates
2 tablespoons brown sugar
1 teaspoon grated orange peel
½ cup orange juice
1 cup margarine or butter, softened
1 cup brown sugar
1 egg
1 teaspoon vanilla
¾ cup flour
¾ cup whole wheat flour
1 cup finely chopped walnuts
½ cup confectioners' sugar
1 tablespoon orange juice

1. In medium saucepan, combine dates, 2 tablespoons brown sugar, orange peel and 1/2 cup orange juice.

2. Bring to a boil; reduce heat and simmer 5 minutes, stirring frequently. Cool filling.

3. In mixing bowl, cream together margarine and 1 cup brown sugar until light and fluffy.

4. Beat in egg and vanilla.

5. Stir in flour, whole wheat flour and walnuts; mix well.

6. Press half of the dough into ungreased 9x13 inch pan.

7. Spread evenly with filling.

8. Drop remaining dough by teaspoonfuls over filling. Gently spread dough evenly over filling.

9. Bake in preheated 350 degree oven 20-30 minutes or until golden brown.

10. To make glaze, combine confectioners' sugar and 1 tablespoon orange juice. Blend until smooth.

11. Spread glaze over warm bars. Allow glaze to set.

12. Cut into bars.

[continued]

ORANGE DATE BARS [continued]

Microwave

> In step **1**, in 2 quart microwave-safe measurer, combine dates, 2 tablespoons brown sugar, orange peel and 1/2 cup orange juice

> In step **2**, microwave on 100% power 3-5 minutes, stirring every minute, until thickened. Cool

APRICOT OATMEAL BARS

[Makes 2 dozen bars]

Bar cookies are a cookie baker's dream because the entire batch of dough is baked at one time. Team that time saving tip with this appealing apricot filling and you'll be baking these bars soon.

1   **cup chopped dried apricots**
½   **cup water**
3   **tablespoons sugar**
¾   **cup quick cooking oats**
⅔   **cup flour**
½   **cup brown sugar**
⅓   **cup margarine or butter**

1. In small saucepan over medium heat, bring apricots, water and sugar to a boil.

2. Reduce heat; cover. Simmer 10 minutes or until apricots are soft and most of the liquid is absorbed. Mash undrained apricots. Cool to room temperature.

3. In mixing bowl, combine oats, flour and brown sugar. Using pastry blender and then finger tips, cut in margarine until mixture is crumbly.

4. Press two thirds crumb mixture into greased 8x8x2 inch baking pan. Spread with apricot mixture. Top with remaining crumb mixture; pat down gently.

5. Bake in preheated 375 degree oven 25 minutes or until golden. Cool on rack.

6. Cut into bars.

7. Store in air tight container.

CINNAMON SAND CRISPS

[Makes 5 to 6 dozen]

When a batch of quick cookies is needed and the ingredient shelf looks depleted, here is a wonderful suggestion. These crispy bar cookies bake in less than half an hour and literally melt in your mouth.

1   **cup butter or margarine, softened**
½   **cup sifted confectioners' sugar**
2   **cups flour**
1   **teaspoon ground cinnamon, divided**
1½ **tablespoons sugar**

1. Cream butter; gradually add confectioners' sugar, beating until light and fluffy.

2. Stir in flour and ½ teaspoon cinnamon.

3. Press or spread dough into lightly greased 10x15 inch jelly roll pan; prick surface with fork tines.

4. Combine 1½ tablespoons sugar and ½ teaspoon cinnamon; sprinkle over dough.

5. Bake in preheated 375 degree oven for 5 minutes.

6. Reduce heat to 300 degrees and bake an additional 20 minutes or until golden brown.

7. Remove cookies from the oven. IMMEDIATELY SCORE into desired bars.

8. Cool in pan. Remove bars and store in tightly covered containers.

CHEESECAKE BARS

[Makes 2-3 dozen bars]

Cheesecake lovers will applaud in appreciation when they taste the creamy texture and mellow flavor of these luscious dessert bars. Just review this recipe.....it's simplicity will cause you to break out in applause too.

5	tablespoons margarine or butter, softened
⅓	cup brown sugar
1	cup flour
¼	cup finely chopped walnuts
1	[8 ounce] package light or regular cream cheese
½	cup sugar
1	egg
2	tablespoons milk
1	tablespoon lemon juice
½	teaspoon vanilla

1. In a mixer bowl, cream together margarine and brown sugar until light and fluffy.

2. Beat in flour and nuts. Set aside 1 cup of this mixture.

3. Press remaining mixture into bottom of ungreased 8x8x2 inch baking pan.

4. Bake in preheated 350 degree oven 12 minutes.

5. Meanwhile, in medium mixing bowl, beat together cream cheese and sugar.

6. Add the egg, milk, lemon juice, and vanilla; beat well.

7. Pour over baked layer in baking pan.

8. Sprinkle reserved flour mixture over top.

9. Bake in 350 degree oven 25 minutes.

10. Cool; cut into bars.

11. Store, covered, in the refrigerator.

PEANUT BUTTER COOKIE BARS

[Makes 4-5 dozen bars]

Kids of all ages like peanut butter and chocolate. In this bar cookie, these flavors prove just why they are so popular. I like to keep a container of these cookies stored in the freezer for spur of the minute sweet treats.

½   **cup margarine or butter, softened**
½   **cup sugar**
½   **cup brown sugar**
1   **egg**
⅓   **cup creamy peanut butter**
½   **teaspoon vanilla**
1   **cup flour**
¼   **teaspoon baking soda**
¼   **teaspoon salt**
1   **cup quick cooking oats**
1   **[6 ounce] package semisweet chocolate morsels**

1. Cream together margarine, sugar, and brown sugar in bowl until light and fluffy with electric mixer at medium speed.

2. Add egg, peanut butter and vanilla; beat well.

3. Sift together flour, baking soda, and salt.

4. Add dry ingredients to creamed mixture, blending well. Stir in oats.

5. Spread mixture in greased 9x13 inch baking pan.

6. Bake in preheated 350 degree oven 25 minutes or until no imprint remains when touched lightly with finger.

7. Remove from oven; sprinkle top with chocolate morsels.

8. Let stand 5 minutes so chocolate can melt. Spread melted chocolate evenly over top. Cool in pan on rack.

9. Cut into bars and store in flat air tight containers.

APPLE PEAR CRISP

[Serves 6-8]

Although the thought of apples and pears reminds me of autumn, this fruit filled dessert is popular any time of the year. Vary the toppings with the season. Serve plain, with whipped topping or try vanilla ice cream or frozen yogurt.

3   cups [3 medium] sliced, peeled apples
3   cups [3 medium] sliced pears
2   tablespoons sugar
4   teaspoons flour
1   teaspoon ground cinnamon
⅛   teaspoon ground nutmeg
1   teaspoon lemon juice
¾   cup flour
1   cup quick cooking rolled oats
¾   cup brown sugar
½   cup margarine or butter

1. In large mixing bowl, combine apples and pears.

2. In small bowl, combine sugar, 4 teaspoons flour, cinnamon and nutmeg. Sprinkle over fruit; toss well.

3. Place fruit mixture in ungreased 2-quart casserole; sprinkle with lemon juice.

4. Combine ¾ cup flour, rolled oats and brown sugar. Using fork or pastry blender, cut in margarine until mixture is crumbled.

5. Sprinkle crumb mixture evenly over fruit.

6. Bake in preheated 375 degree oven 35-45 minutes or until golden brown and fruit is tender.

Microwave

In step **3**, use microwave-safe casserole

In step **4**, use dark brown sugar.

In step **6**, microwave on 100% power 12-15 minutes, rotating casserole once, until fruit is tender.

FRESH STRAWBERRY PIE

[Serves 6-8]

Few family members and friends can resist bright red slices of fresh strawberry pie. Not only are the eye appeal and flavor irresistible, the surprise bonus is that it is sugar-free.

1   [6 ounce] can unsweetened frozen apple juice concentrate, thawed [¾ cup]
1   quart fresh strawberries
1   [0.3 ounce] package sugar-free strawberry gelatin
1   baked 9 inch pastry shell

1. Pour thawed apple juice concentrate into 1 quart measurer.
2. Wash, hull and slice strawberries.
3. Puree enough strawberries in food processor or blender that when added to the apple juice concentrate makes just slightly less that 2 cups of liquid.
4. Heat in saucepan until bubbling hot.
5. Add gelatin and stir thoroughly to dissolve.
6. Chill until slightly thickened.
7. Gently fold remaining strawberries into gelatin mixture.
8. Pour mixture into cooled pastry shell.
9. Chill until firm.
10. At serving time, cut into attractive slices. Top with Lowfat Topping using the recipe also on this page.

Microwave

In step **1**, use microwave-safe measurer.

In step **4**, microwave on 100% power 3-4 minutes, stirring once.

LOWFAT WHIPPED TOPPING

[Serves 12-15]

Evaporated skim milk is a wonderful friend to all those interested in reducing fat intake. This lowfat topping is not as stable as traditional whipped cream, but the reduction in fat grams and calories is well worth the inconvenience.

[continued]

Lowfat Whipped Topping [continued]

⅔ cup evaporated skim milk
3 tablespoons confectioners' sugar
1 teaspoon vanilla

1. Place small straight sided bowl and beaters in the freezer to chill.

2. Pour evaporated skim milk into flat pan; freeze until slushy.

3. Spoon partially frozen skim milk into chilled small bowl.

4. Beat with chilled beaters until fluffy.

5. Add confectioners' sugar and vanilla; beat until soft peaks form, scraping bowl occasionally.

6. Serve immediately over favorite dessert or hold it in the freezer for up to 20 minutes.

Vegetable Oil Pastry

[Makes one 9 inch pastry shell]

As we become more and more concerned about the consumption of saturated fat, an oil pastry recipe is mandatory. I think the addition of the egg white creates an exceptional pastry shell. It works great with the Fresh Strawberry Pie on page 200.

1⅓ cups flour
¼ teaspoon salt
1 egg white, slightly beaten
⅓ cup vegetable oil
1 tablespoon ice water

1. In medium mixing bowl, combine flour and salt.

2. In small bowl, combine egg white, oil and water.

3. Add liquid ingredients to flour. Stir with a fork until dry ingredients are moistened.

4. Shape into a ball; place between 2 sheets of waxed paper.

5. Roll to a 12 inch circle.

6. Place in a 9 inch pieplate; flute edges.

7. Generously prick bottom and sides of pastry with a fork.

8. Bake in preheated 450 degree oven for about 12 minutes or until lightly browned.

RHUBARB CREAM PIE

[Serves 6-8]

For many folks rhubarb is one of the "comfort foods" of spring. Since my husband, George, is part of this group he welcomes the aroma of this wonderful pie baking in the oven. He knows that very soon he can sample one of his favorite rites of spring.

1½ cups sugar
¼ cup flour
¾ teaspoon ground nutmeg
3 slightly beaten eggs
4 cups sliced fresh rhubarb
1 [9 inch] single-crust unbaked pastry shell
½ cup flour
¼ cup sugar
⅓ cup margarine or butter

1. In large mixing bowl, stir together the 1 and 1/2 cups sugar, 1/4 cup flour and nutmeg.

2. Add the eggs and blend well.

3. Gently stir in the rhubarb.

4. Turn the mixture into prepared pastry shell.

5. In small bowl, stir together the 1/2 cup flour and 1/4 cup sugar.

6. Cut in margarine or butter until mixture resembles coarse crumbs. Sprinkle over the top of the pie.

7. Cover edge of pie with foil to prevent overbrowning.

8. Bake in preheated 400 degree oven for 20 minutes. Remove foil.

9. Continue baking 20-30 minutes more until topping is golden and pie is set.

MICHIGAN CHERRY PIE

[Serve 6-8]

Whenever our nephew, David Howell, comes from Dallas, Texas for a visit in Michigan, he enjoys a pie baking session. Since he is partial to cherry pie, we usually start with this recipe.

Pastry for 2-crust pie
2   **[16 ounce] cans pitted tart cherries [water pack]**
2½ **tablespoons quick-cooking tapioca**
¼   **teaspoon salt**
¼   **teaspoon almond extract**
1   **teaspoon lemon juice**
4   **drops red food color, if desired**
1¼ **cups sugar**
1   **tablespoon margarine or butter**

1. Drain cherries, reserving some of the liquid.

2. Measure ⅓ cup cherry liquid into mixing bowl. Add tapioca, salt, almond extract, lemon juice and food color. Mix lightly.

3. Add cherries and 1 cup sugar. Mix and let stand while rolling out pastry.

4. Roll out pastry. Fit pastry into bottom of 9 inch pie pan. Trim ½ inch beyond outer rim of pan.

5. Fill pastry with cherry mixture.

6. Dot with margarine. Sprinkle with remaining ¼ cup sugar.

7. Moisten rim with water.

8. Adjust latticed top; flute edges. [To keep high rim from browning faster than crisscross strips, circle pie with a stand-up foil collar. Fold foil rim and leave on during entire baking.]

9. Bake in preheated 425 degree oven 40-45 minutes until liquid is thickened and bubbly.

10. Remove from oven. Cool.

Microwave

In step **4**, use microwave-safe pie plate.

In step **9**, elevate pie on microwave roasting rack. Microwave on 100% power 8-12 minutes, rotating after 5 minutes. Put pie in preheated 425 degree oven. Bake 15-20 minutes until pie is golden brown in color and juice bubbles up, appearing thick.

SOUR CREAM LIME TART

[Serves 8]

How happy I am that I was introduced to this elegant mouth watering pie by my friend, Joanne Littig. Of course, I'm even happier that she generously shared this treasured family recipe with me and now with you.

¼	cup unsalted butter
1	cup sugar
3	tablespoons cornstarch
1	tablespoon finely grated lime peel
1	cup whipping cream
1	cup sour cream
1	9 inch butter crumb or graham cracker crust
½	cup whipping cream
2	tablespoons sugar
¼	teaspoon vanilla
6	tablespoons sour cream
	Lime slices for garnish, if desired

1. In heavy saucepan over low heat, melt butter.

2. Add 1 cup sugar, cornstarch, lime peel and 1 cup whipping cream.

3. Bring to a boil, whisking constantly with a wire whisk.

4. Reduce to simmer and continue stirring until thick and smooth.

5. Cool to room temperature, stirring occasionally.

6. Fold in 1 cup sour cream and spread evenly in prepared crust.

7. For topping, whip ½ cup whipping cream until it starts to thicken. Add 2 tablespoons sugar and vanilla; whip until soft peaks form.

8. Fold in 6 tablespoons sour cream.

9. Spread topping over filling.

10. Chill at least 4 hours before serving. At serving time, garnish each serving with a lime slice, if desired.

LIGHT LEMON ANGEL TORTE

[Serves 12-16]

This lovely lemon torte is light in calories and low in fat. Depending on the season, your flavor buds and/or desired color scheme, this dessert can be topped with any fresh fruit or cooked fruit topping.

1   [8 or 9 ounce] angel food cake
1   [3 ounce] package lemon flavored gelatin
½   cup boiling water
⅓   cup frozen lemonade concentrate, thawed
1   [12 ounce] can evaporated skim milk [1⅔ cups]

1. Spray an eight inch baking dish or pan with non-stick vegetable spray.

2. Cut angel food cake in 1 inch cubes. There should be about 4 cups of cake cubes. Arrange cake cubes in prepared dish.

3. In large bowl, dissolve gelatin in boiling water.

4. Stir in lemonade concentrate and evaporated skim milk.

5. Refrigerate until gelatin mixture mounds, about 1 hour.

6. Beat mixture, until very light and fluffy, with electric mixer.

7. Pour mixture over cake cubes. Refrigerate until firm.

8. Cut into squares and serve with favorite fruit sauce or topping.

FRUIT FANTASY PUFF

[Serves 6-8]

This elegant, but easy, pastry topped cream puff is the perfect showcase for fresh fruit. Even though the procedure appears long, the preparation time is very manageable. The mouth watering results are the proof of the pudding.

⅔ **cup flour**
⅓ **cup margarine or butter, chilled**
2-4 **teaspoons ice water**
½ **cup water**
¼ **cup margarine or butter**
½ **cup flour**
2   **eggs**
1½ **cups cold milk**
1   **[3.5 oz.] package instant vanilla pudding and pie filling**
½ **cup whipping cream, whipped or 1 cup whipped topping**
1½- 2 **cups fresh fruit, such as blueberries, raspberries, strawberries, grapes, or sliced peaches**

1. Put ⅔ cup flour in mixing bowl. Cut in ⅓ cup margarine with pastry blender or fork until particles are the size of small peas.

2. Sprinkle with ice water, 1 teaspoonful at a time, mixing lightly with fork until flour mixture is moistened and soft dough forms.

3. On parchment lined or ungreased cookie sheet, press dough into an 8 inch circle. [I like to use parchment paper and draw an eight inch circle as a guide.]

4. In medium saucepan over medium heat, heat ½ cup water and ¼ cup margarine to boiling.

5. Stir in ½ cup flour, stirring vigorously until mixture leaves sides of pan in smooth ball.

6. Remove from heat.

7. Add eggs, one at a time, beating vigorously after each, until mixture is smooth and glossy.

8. Spoon puff dough onto crust. With back of spoon, make a deep well in center, building up sides and shaping into a shell.

9. Bake in preheated 375 degree oven for 20 minutes. Remove from oven; with fork, prick center of shell.

[continued]

FRUIT FANTASY PUFF [continued]

10. Return to oven and bake 20-30 minutes or until deep golden brown and puffy. Cool completely.

11. In medium bowl, combine milk and pudding mix; beat at low speed of electric mixer 1 minute.

12. Chill 15 minutes or until set; fold in whipped cream or topping.

13. To assemble for serving, slide puff shell onto serving plate.

14. Layer cream mixture and fruit into puff shell.

15. Refrigerate until serving; cut into wedges to serve.

16. Garnish with additional fruit, if desired.

BERRIED TREASURE

[Serves 8]

Hidden beneath this white creamy layer, you'll find strawberry slices just waiting to be discovered. It's a contrast in flavor and texture designed to be remembered.

6   ounces of light or regular cream cheese, softened
1   cup [8 ounces] light or regular sour cream
⅓   cup light brown sugar
1   quart fresh strawberries, sliced and chilled
3   tablespoons light brown sugar

1. Combine cream cheese, sour cream, and ⅓ cup brown sugar. Beat at medium speed of an electric mixer until smooth. Chill 1-2 hours, if time permits.

2. Place strawberries in pretty serving bowl or individual compotes or dessert dishes.

3. Just before serving, top with cream cheese mixture. Sprinkle with 3 tablespoons brown sugar.

Strawberry Lemon Cheesecake

[Serves 8]

This cheesecake is a way to show off the principle of draining yogurt into yogurt cheese as described on page 270. It does require remembering to drain the yogurt the day before you make the cheesecake, but it's an extremely simple procedure. Here's to your happy healthy heart.

4   cups lemon yogurt, drained to 2 cups lemon yogurt cheese
¼   cup sugar
1   tablespoon cornstarch
4   egg whites
½   teaspoon grated lemon peel
2   cups sliced fresh strawberries, sweetened, if desired

1. Drain lemon yogurt into lemon yogurt cheese using the method described on page 270.

2. In large bowl, whisk together yogurt cheese, sugar and cornstarch.

3. Lightly beat egg whites.

4. Add egg whites and lemon peel to cheese mixture. Whisk until blended.

5. Spray 9 inch pie plate with vegetable cooking spray.

6. Pour mixture into prepared pan and smooth the top with a spatula.

7. Bake in preheated 325 degree oven 25-35 minutes until center is set.

8. Cool slightly on a wire rack. Refrigerate until chilled.

9. To serve, cut into small slices and top with fresh strawberries.

Melon Raspberry Sundae

[Serves 6-8]

The next time you see tempting cantaloupe in the produce section of the grocery store or at a local fresh air fruit market, remember this triple treat dessert. I think you'll agree with me that the red raspberry sauce cascades over the melon and frozen yogurt in picture perfect fashion.

[continued]

MELON RASPBERRY SUNDAE [continued]

2   teaspoons cornstarch
2   tablespoons water
¼   cup currant jelly
1   [10 ounce] package frozen raspberries, thawed & undrained
1   cantaloupe, peeled, cut into wedges
1   quart vanilla frozen yogurt or ice milk

1. In small saucepan, combine cornstarch and water; blend until smooth.

2. Add jelly and raspberries.

3. Cook over medium heat until sauce boils and thickens, stirring occasionally. Cool.

4. At serving time, arrange cantaloupe wedges and scoops of frozen yogurt on individual serving plates or in bowls.

5. Spoon raspberry sauce over melon and frozen yogurt.

HIDDEN TREASURE MERINGUES

[Serves 6]

Underneath these feather light mounds of meringue, sponge cake surprises can be found. The kiwi fruit topping on page 246 is one of my favorite ways to serve this picture pretty dessert.

4   egg whites
¼   teaspoon cream of tartar
½   cup sugar
6   individual sponge cake cups

1. Line cookie sheet with parchment paper or foil.

2. In large bowl, beat egg whites and cream of tartar until soft peaks form.

3. Gradually add sugar, beating until stiff peaks form.

4. Arrange sponge cake cups 3 inches apart on prepared cookie sheet.

5. Evenly spread meringue over top and sides of sponge cake cups; make indentation in meringue in center of each cup.

6. Bake in preheated 350 degree oven 10-15 minutes or until meringue is light golden brown.

7. Cool; serve with favorite fruit topping.

ANGEL FOOD TRIFLE

[Serves 15]

The next time you need a lowfat dessert for a crowd, please consider this lovely layered trifle. It's a lighter version of the traditionally rich dessert. Angel food cake replaces buttery pound cake or macaroons and the custard is made with skim milk and vanilla low-fat yogurt rather than richer milk products.

⅓   cup sugar
¼   cup cornstarch
¼   teaspoon salt
2   cups skim milk
¼   cup egg substitute
1   teaspoon grated lemon rind
¼   cup lemon juice
2   [8 ounce] cartons vanilla low-fat yogurt
1   [11-13 ounce] angel food cake
2   cups sliced fresh strawberries
3   kiwi fruit, sliced
     Strawberries for garnish

1. Combine sugar, cornstarch and salt in a saucepan; gradually add milk, stirring well.

2. Cook over medium heat until mixture begins to thicken, stirring constantly.

3. Remove from heat; gradually add egg substitute, stirring constantly with a wire whisk.

4. Cook over medium-low heat 2 minutes, stirring constantly.

5. Remove from heat; cool slightly.

6. Stir in lemon rind and lemon juice; chill.

7. Beat or stir cream mixture until smooth. Fold yogurt into cream mixture.

8. Tear or cut angel food cake into bite-size pieces.

9. Place one-third of cake in bottom of a 16-cup trifle bowl or other pretty bowl.

10. Spoon one-third of custard over cake; arrange half each of strawberry slices and kiwi slices around lower edge of bowl and over custard.

[continued]

ANGEL FOOD TRIFLE   [continued]

11. Repeat procedure with remaining ingredients, ending with strawberries as garnish.

12. Cover and chill at least 3 or 4 hours.

Microwave

In step **1**, combine sugar, cornstarch and salt in 2 quart microwave-safe measurer; gradually add milk, stirring well.

In step **2**, microwave on 100% power 4-6 minutes, stirring three or four times, until mixture begins to thicken.

In step **4**, microwave on 80% power 1-2 minutes, stirring once.

FRESH STRAWBERRY SAUCE 'N FRUIT

[Serves 4]

I always have been partial to recipes which have a short ingredient list, but are long on flavor. This quick plan turns fresh strawberries into a pretty sauce worthy of any occasion.

1   **cup sliced fresh strawberries**
¼   **cup orange juice**
3   **tablespoons sugar**
2   **bananas, sliced**
1   **[20 ounce] can juice pack pineapple tidbits, drained**
½   **cup blueberries for garnish, if desired**

1. In food processor container with steel blade or blender, combine strawberries, orange juice and sugar.

2. Blend until smooth.

3. In pretty bowl or four individual sauce dishes, layer bananas and pineapple.

4. Drizzle with strawberry sauce.

5. Garnish with blueberries, if desired

PINEAPPLE CREAMSICLES

[Serves 6]

This frozen treat is dedicated to all parents and grandparents who like to have healthy snacks to serve at a moment's notice. After these yogurt pops have frozen, keep them stored in a self-sealing plastic freezer bag for easy access.

2 [8 ounce] cartons strawberry or banana lowfat yogurt
1 [8 ounce] can juice pack crushed pineapple, undrained
6 [5 ounce] cold drink cups
6 wooden popsicle sticks

1. In food processor bowl with metal blade or blender container, combine yogurt and pineapple; process until smooth.

2. Fill drink cups with yogurt mixture; insert sticks.

3. Freeze until firm. Store in airtight bags.

4. To serve, remove drink cups.

ORANGE MARBLE FREEZE

[Serves 12-16]

As with most frozen desserts, this orange sherbet and vanilla ice cream creation is a make ahead friend to all busy cooks. Just keep it, well covered, in the freezer for unexpected guests.

CRUST:

½ cup margarine or butter
1 cup flour
¼ cup sugar
½ cup coconut

FILLING:

1 quart orange sherbet, softened
1 quart vanilla ice cream, softened
Mandarin orange segments for garnish, if desired

1. In large skillet, melt margarine.

2. Add flour, sugar and coconut to melted margarine.

[continued]

ORANGE MARBLE FREEZE [continued]

3. Cook over medium-high heat for 4-8 minutes or until mixture is medium golden brown and crumbly, stirring constantly.

4. Reserve ¼ cup crumbs mixture for topping.

5. Press remaining warm crumb mixture firmly in bottom of 9 inch square pan.

6. In large bowl, combine sherbet and ice cream, swirling to marble.

7. Spread filling on prepared crust.

8. Sprinkle with remaining crumbs.

9. Cover; freeze several hours or until firm.

10. Let stand at room temperature a few minutes before serving.

11. To serve, cut into squares.

12. Garnish with mandarin orange segments, if desired.

RAINBOW SHERBET DESSERT

[Serves 8-12]

I've always liked this "waxed paper" way to remove a refrigerated or frozen dessert from a loaf pan. In this recipe, attractive layers of sherbet are frozen together in picture pretty fashion.

1 **pint lime sherbet, slightly softened**
2 **tablespoons chopped toasted almonds**
1 **pint pineapple sherbet, softened**
1 **pint raspberry sherbet softened**
Large fresh strawberries for garnish, if desired

1. Line an 8x4 inch loaf pan with waxed paper, extending paper beyond rim.

2. In medium mixing bowl, combine lime sherbet and almonds; spread in bottom of prepared pan. Cover and freeze 30 minutes.

3. Spread pineapple sherbet evenly over lime sherbet mixture; cover and freeze 30 minutes.

4. Spread raspberry sherbet evenly over pineapple sherbet; cover and freeze until firm.

5. At serving time, invert dessert on platter and remove waxed paper.

6. Cut in 1 inch slices.

7. Garnish with fresh strawberries, if desired.

FROSTY PUMPKIN PIE

[Serves 8-10]

Here is a pumpkin pie that may easily become a permanent part of your holiday menu plans. Traditional pumpkin flavor is captured in this freezer friendly pie.

1½ **cups crushed gingersnap cookies**
¼ **cup margarine or butter, melted**
1   **[16 ounce] can pumpkin [2 cups]**
1   **pint vanilla ice cream or frozen yogurt, softened**
1   **cup confectioners' sugar**
1½ **teaspoons pumpkin pie spice**
⅛ **teaspoon salt, if desired**
1   **teaspoon vanilla**
2   **cups frozen whipped topping**

1. In small bowl, combine gingersnap crumbs with melted margarine; mix well.

2. Reserve 2 tablespoons crumb mixture for topping.

3. Press mixture evenly in bottom and up sides of 9 inch pie pan; refrigerate.

4. In large bowl, combine pumpkin, ice cream, confectioners sugar, pumpkin pie spice, salt and vanilla; stir until smooth. [Use whisk or beater, if you wish.]

5. Fold whipped topping into pumpkin mixture.

6. Pour mixture into prepared crust.

7. Top with reserved 2 tablespoons crumbs.

8. Freeze several hours or until firm. Cover tightly.

9. Let stand at room temperature a short time before serving.

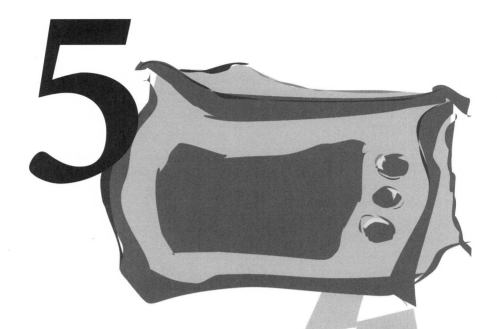

5

Microwave

Now that microwave ovens have come of age, most cooks have the option of using this quick and effecient method of food prepration.

These significant microwave recipes have been carefully selected and tested to help you take advantage of the marvels of microwave cooking. More than half of the recipes feature less fat, sugar or salt.

Contents

ORIENTAL APPETIZER MEATBALLS

[Makes 3-4 dozen meatballs]

It's so easy to make meatballs when a microwave oven is involved. Gone are the days when meatballs stick to the pan and need to be carefully watched. This clever variation has a crunchy surprise inside each morsel.

1	**pound lean ground beef**
2	**tablespoons dry bread crumbs**
¼	**teaspoon ground ginger**
¼	**teaspoon garlic powder**
⅛	**teaspoon ground pepper**
1	**tablespoon sodium reduced soy sauce**
1	**[8 ounce] can whole water chestnuts, drained and quartered**
1	**tablespoon low sugar orange marmalade**

1. Combine ground beef, bread crumbs, ginger, garlic powder, pepper and soy sauce. Mix thoroughly.

2. Shape about a tablespoon of meat mixture around a quartered water chestnut, forming a ball.

3. Arrange meat balls on rack in 8x12 inch microwave-safe baking dish. Cover with waxed paper.

4. Microwave on 100% power 4-6 minute or until almost cooked, rotating dish once. Drain.

5. In small microwave-safe dish, melt orange marmalade on 100% power for 30-45 seconds.

6. Toss melted marmalade with meatballs.

7. Heat meatballs, covered with waxed paper, on 100% power for 1-2 minutes or until piping hot.

8. Serve on frilly toothpicks.

CHEESY POTATO SNACKS

[Makes 24 appetizers]

The next time you see small new potatoes at the Farmer's Market or your favorite supermarket, remember this healthy snack idea. It will especially please family members and friends who are partial to potatoes.

12 small new potatoes, halved
2 tablespoons water
½ cup flavored Cheddar cheese spread
Toppings like, parsley sprigs, pimento slice or chopped pecans

1. Place potatoes, cut side down, in 8x12 inch microwave safe baking dish. Add water.

2. Cover with vented plastic wrap.

3. Microwave on 100% power 7-10 minutes or until potatoes are tender, rotating dish once half way through cooking. [Remember that the guideline for cooking potatoes in the microwave is 6-7 minutes per pound.]

4. Let stand 3 minutes; drain.

5. Cool slightly.

6. On cut side of each potato, place about 1 teaspoonful cheese spread.

7. Top with parsley, pimento or chopped pecan.

8. Serve warm.

CHICKEN NUGGETS

[Makes 25-30 nuggets]

Actually these tasty bites of chicken could be served as an appetizer or snack as well as a light entree. It's a great idea to serve hungry kids. In fact, get them to help with the entire procedure...most kids love to cook.

1	**pound skinned and boned chicken breast**
3	**tablespoons skim milk**
¼	**cup dry bread crumbs**
¼	**cup grated Parmesan cheese**
½	**teaspoon seasoned salt**
½	**teaspoon paprika**
⅛	**teaspoon garlic powder**
⅛	**teaspoon pepper**
	Barbecue sauce or sweet and sour sauce for dipping

1. Cut the chicken into 1-inch cubes. Place the pieces in a small bowl.

2. Pour milk over chicken. Mix lightly so that all chicken is coated with milk.

3. In a plastic bag, combine bread crumbs, Parmesan cheese, seasoned salt, paprika, garlic powder and pepper. Shake until ingredients are evenly combined.

4. Put half the pieces in the bag. Shake the bag to evenly coat the chicken. Arrange these chicken pieces in a circle on a microwave-safe plate. Cover with paper towel.

5. Microwave on plate on 100% power for 3-4 minutes, rotating the plate once. Chicken should not be pink inside when done.

6. Repeat procedure with other half of the chicken pieces.

7. Arrange chicken nuggets on serving plate. Enjoy with the dipping sauce of your choice, if desired.

MEXICAN CHICKEN BREASTS

[Serves 2]

I found and tested this recipe when I was writing a foods column for The Grand Rapids Press. The recipes that I was sharing were adapted for persons cooking in the microwave oven for one or two. We like this chicken so much that now I double or triple the recipe depending on how many I wish to serve. Remember the microwave timings are then doubled or tripled too.

2   **tablespoons dry bread crumbs**
1   **tablespoon grated Parmesan cheese**
½   **teaspoon chili powder**
1   **tablespoon margarine**
1   **skinned boneless chicken breast, cut in half [8 ounces]**
2   **tablespoons salsa or picante sauce**
¼   **cup shredded Monterey Jack cheese**

1. Combine bread crumbs, Parmesan cheese, and chili powder on a piece of waxed paper. Set aside.

2. In microwave-safe 9 inch pie plate, microwave margarine on 100% power about 30 seconds or until melted.

3. Coat chicken pieces on both sides with margarine, then roll in crumbs. Return chicken to pie plate. Cover with paper towel.

4. Microwave on 100% power for 3 minutes or until chicken is partially cooked.

5. Spread salsa or picante over chicken pieces. Sprinkle cheese over chicken.

6. Microwave on 100% power, uncovered, 1 and 1/2 to 2 minutes or until chicken is done and cheese is melted.

BARBECUED CHICKEN

[Serves 6]

As we consume more and more chicken, creative cooks are always on the look out for yet another way to serve this favorite entree to family and friends. In this recipe, eight carefully measured familiar ingredients become a wonderful barbecue sauce for boneless chicken breasts.

3	**tablespoons brown sugar**
3	**tablespoons ketchup**
2	**tablespoons chili sauce**
1	**tablespoon vinegar**
2	**teaspoons lemon juice**
2	**teaspoons Worcestershire sauce**
½	**teaspoon salt**
⅛	**teaspoon ground pepper**
6	**skinned, boneless chicken breast halves**

1. In 2 cup microwave-safe measurer, combine brown sugar, ketchup, chili sauce, vinegar, lemon juice, Worcestershire sauce, salt and pepper.

2. Microwave, uncovered, on 100% power for 1-2 minutes or until mixture boils; set aside.

3. Arrange chicken in an 8x12 inch microwave-safe baking dish with thickest portions toward the outside of the dish.

4. Cover with waxed paper. Microwave on 100% power for 10 minutes, rotating dish once. Drain and rearrange chicken.

5. Brush chicken with sauce.

6. Cover again with waxed paper. Microwave on 100% power 9-10 minutes or until chicken is done and glazed, rearranging chicken once or twice.

7. Let stand 5 minutes before serving.

ORIENTAL MICROWAVE GRILLED CHICKEN

[Serves 4-5]

It may seem unusual to find a grill recipe in the microwave chapter, but I'm convinced that the easiest way to barbecue poultry is to use the microwave for precooking. Add this interesting flavorful sauce and you'll be known as the "Grilled Chicken Guru".

¼   **cup soy sauce**
2   **tablespoons prepared mustard**
1   **tablespoon honey**
1   **tablespoon lemon juice**
¼   **teaspoon ground ginger**
3   **pounds meaty chicken pieces, skinned if desired**

1. In 1 cup glass measuring cup, combine soy sauce and mustard. Mix well.

2. Add honey, lemon juice and ginger. Thoroughly combine mixture.

3. Rinse chicken and pat dry with paper towel.

4. Put chicken in resealable plastic bag or flat dish.

5. Pour sauce over chicken and refrigerate 1-2 hours to develop flavor.

6. Remove from marinade and place in 8x12 inch microwave-safe dish. Cover with waxed paper.

7. Microwave on 100% power 15 minutes, rotating dish halfway through cooking time. [The guideline is 5 minutes per pound of chicken on 100% power in the microwave oven.]

8. Barbecue about 4 inches above hot coals 15-20 minutes or until golden brown, turning occasionally and brushing with marinade.

BARBECUED CHICKEN SANDWICHES

[Serves 4 or 5]

To be truthful, this dynamite barbecued sandwich idea is the first time I've prepared a recipe that teams salsa with barbecue sauce. The flavors compliment each other so well, this casual entree may soon become a specialty of your house.

1½ **cups finely chopped cooked chicken**
½ **cup thick salsa, mild, medium or hot**
½ **cup barbecue sauce**
2 **tablespoons sliced green onions**
4-5 **hamburger buns, split & toasted**

1. In 2 quart microwave-safe casserole, combine chicken, salsa, barbecue sauce and green onions; mix well.

2. Cover with lid or vented plastic wrap.

3. Microwave on 100% power 4-5 minutes or until mixture is thoroughly heated, stirring two or three times.

4. Serve on toasted buns.

TEX-MEX TURKEY

[Serves 6-8]

Ground turkey is a popular lowfat source of protein. In this recipe, pungent south of the border flavors enhance the mild characteristics of turkey. The result is an entree that will easily win approval with family members of all ages.

1   **pound ground raw turkey**
2   **[8 ounce] cans tomato sauce**
1   **teaspoon chili powder**
½   **teaspoon ground cumin**
¼   **teaspoon salt**
¼   **teaspoon garlic powder**
    Flour tortillas
    Shredded lettuce
    Chopped tomato
    Shredded lowfat yellow cheese

1. Spray hard plastic colander with vegetable cooking spray to prevent sticking. Put ground turkey in colander and rest colander in microwave-safe pie plate.

2. Microwave turkey on 100% power 5-7 minutes, breaking up meat once with fork.

3. In 2 quart microwave-safe casserole, combine drained cooked turkey, tomato sauce, chili powder, cumin, salt and garlic powder.

4. Microwave on 100% power 8-10 minutes, stirring mixture two times.

5. Heat tortillas according to package directions.

6. In warm tortilla, layer meat mixture, shredded lettuce, chopped tomato and shredded cheese. Roll up tortilla.

7. Enjoy.

FISH CREOLE

[Serves 4]

I often get requests for fish recipes that are fast and flavorful. Keeping that criteria in mind, here is my number one suggestion. This perfectly spiced tomato sauce base is a great way to enhance mild fish fillets.

½   **cup diced celery**
½   **cup chopped green pepper**
1   **small onion, thinly sliced**
1   **[8 ounce] can tomato sauce**
½   **teaspoon chili powder**
¼   **teaspoon salt**
¼   **teaspoon garlic powder**
¼   **teaspoon dried oregano leaves**
¼   **teaspoon dried thyme leaves**
1   **pound mild flavored fish fillets, like cod or sole**

1. Combine celery, green pepper and onion in a 1½ quart shallow microwave-safe dish. Cover with vented plastic wrap.

2. Microwave on 100% power 2-3 minutes or until just about tender.

3. Add tomato sauce, chili powder, salt, garlic, oregano and thyme to vegetable mixture. Cover with vented plastic wrap.

4. Microwave on 100% power 2-3 minutes or until mixture boils.

5. Push vegetables to side of dish; arrange fillets in dish.

6. Spoon vegetables and sauce over fish. Again, cover with vented plastic wrap.

7. Microwave on 100% power 4-6 minutes or until fish flakes apart easily, rotating dish once.

8. Garnish with fresh parsley and enjoy.

FISH FILLETS AU GRATIN

[Serves 3-4]

Fish fillets cook so quickly in the microwave oven, lots of cooks set the table before they start to cook fish entrees. In this recipe, I often transfer the fillets to a microwave-safe serving platter before adding the cheese. That way it's all ready to serve when the cheese has melted.

1	**pound fresh or frozen fish fillets, thawed**
1	**tablespoon lemon juice**
1	**tablespoon chopped fresh parsley or 1 teaspoon dried parsley**
½	**teaspoon onion salt**
½	**teaspoon paprika**
⅛	**teaspoon pepper**
½	**cup shredded American cheese**

1. Place fish in 8x12 inch microwave-safe baking dish.

2. Sprinkle with lemon juice, parsley, onion salt, paprika and pepper.

3. Cover with vented plastic wrap.

4. Microwave on 100% power 5-7 minutes or until fish flakes easily with a fork, rotating dish once.

5. Remove plastic wrap; drain well. If desired, put fish fillets on microwave-safe serving platter.

6. Sprinkle with cheese; microwave on 100% power 45-60 seconds or until cheese is melted.

BREADED ORANGE ROUGHY

[Serves 3-4]

Orange roughy is a popular fish that's readily available in the frozen food case or thawed, for your convenience, at the fresh fish counter of large supermarkets. The flavorful breading mixture in this recipe creates a light crispy coating that's preferred by folks who like dry rather than moist fish.

¾   **cup crushed seasoned croutons**
¼   **cup grated Parmesan cheese**
2   **teaspoons dried parsley flakes**
¼   **teaspoon paprika**
2   **egg whites**
1   **tablespoon water**
1   **tablespoon lemon juice**
1   **pound frozen orange roughy, thawed**

1. On piece of waxed paper, combine crushed croutons, Parmesan cheese; parsley flakes and paprika; blend well.

2. In a shallow dish, combine egg whites, water and lemon juice; blend well.

3. Cut fish into serving size pieces.

4. Dip fish pieces in egg mixture; coat with crouton mixture.

5. Tuck thin ends of fish under to form pieces of uniform thickness.

6. Place fish on microwave-safe roasting rack.

7. Microwave on 100% power 5-7 minutes or until fish flakes easily with a fork, rotating dish once.

LEMON HERBED SOLE

[Serves 3-4]

Fresh thyme enhances the mild flavor of sole fillets. It can usually be purchased year-round in the produce section of large supermarkets. Of course, dried thyme leaves can also be used.

1   **cup thin julienne sliced carrots**
2   **tablespoons water**
1   **pound fresh or frozen sole fillets, thawed**
2   **green onions, sliced**
1   **tablespoon margarine, melted**
1   **tablespoon lemon juice**
1   **teaspoon chopped fresh thyme or ¼ teaspoon dried thyme leaves, crushed**
½   **teaspoon salt**

1. Place carrots and water in 1 quart microwave-safe casserole; cover with lid or vented plastic wrap.

2. Microwave on 100% power 2-3 minutes or until carrots are crisp-tender; drain.

3. Place fish fillets in 8x12 inch microwave-safe baking dish.

4. Arrange carrots and green onions over fish.

5. In small bowl, combine margarine and lemon juice; drizzle over fish and vegetables.

6. Sprinkle with thyme.

7. Cover with vented plastic wrap.

8. Microwave on 100% power 5-7 minutes or until fish flakes easily with a fork, rotating dish once.

9. Sprinkle with salt and serve.

FISH 'N VEGETABLE MEDLEY IN PARCHMENT

[Serves 2]

For years classy cooks have created culinary combinations in parchment paper. Now, as we focus on healthy food preparation, this method of cooking has come of age in the microwave oven.

Parchment paper or non-stick microwave cooking paper
½ **cup quartered cherry tomatoes**
3 **tablespoons sliced green onions**
1 **tablespoon lemon juice**
½ **teaspoon dill weed**
¼ **pound fresh snow peas or ½ [6 ounce] package frozen pea pods, thawed**
½ **pound mild fish fillets, like scrod cod or orange roughy Lemon pepper, if desired**

1. Cut two 12x15 inch pieces of parchment paper; fold in half lengthwise, creasing firmly. Trim each piece into a heart like shape. Set aside.

2. Combine tomatoes, green onions, lemon juice and dill weed.

3. Arrange snow peas attractively on half of each parchment heart, near crease.

4. Sprinkle fish fillets with lemon pepper, if desired, and arrange over snow peas.

5. Spoon tomato mixture over fish fillets.

6. Fold over remaining parchment halves of hearts. Starting with rounded edge of heart, pleat and crimp edges together to seal. Twist end tightly.

7. Put parchment packets on large microwave-safe plate.

8. Microwave on 100% power 5-7 minutes or until fish flakes apart easily with fork. Let stand a few minutes. Enjoy.

SEAFOOD VEGETABLE MEDLEY

[Serves 4-5]

Microwave users have always been enthusiastic about recipes that could be cooked and served in the same dish. If it's an entree complete in itself, the enthusiasm becomes almost euphoric. To complete the menu, just add fresh fruit and an interesting bread product.

4   ounces uncooked macaroni shells [about 1 cup]
2   cups sliced fresh mushrooms
2   cups fresh broccoli pieces
1   cup thinly sliced carrots
⅛   teaspoon garlic powder
1   tablespoon margarine
     Water
1½ teaspoons cornstarch
2   teaspoons instant chicken bouillon
½   teaspoon lemon juice
8   ounces frozen imitation crabmeat sticks, thawed

1. Cook macaroni shells according to package directions. Drain, rinse, and set aside.

2. Combine mushrooms, broccoli, carrots, garlic powder and margarine in 2 quart microwave-safe casserole.

3. Cover with lid or plastic wrap that is vented.

4. Microwave on 100% power 8-9 minutes or until vegetables are crisp-tender, stirring once.

5. Thoroughly drain vegetables, reserving liquid.

6. Put liquid in 1 quart microwave-safe measurer. Add water to make ¾ cup. Mix in cornstarch, chicken bouillon and lemon juice. Stir until blended.

7. Microwave on 100% power, uncovered, 1-2 minutes or until mixture boils and thickens, stirring every 30 seconds.

8. In original casserole, combine cooked vegetables, sauce and macaroni.

9. Cut crabmeat sticks into 1 inch pieces; add to sauce. Mix lightly.

10. Microwave on 100% power, uncovered, 2-3 minutes or until heated thoroughly.

Speedy Beefy Noodle Soup

[Serves 4]

For this quick soup, lean ground beef, instant beef bouillon and the microwave oven cooperate beautifully to produce an entree long on flavor, but short on preparation time. Sometimes, I use leftover cooked vegetables rather than the frozen mixture.

½   **pound lean ground beef**
2   **tablespoons chopped onion**
4   **cups water**
½   **cup uncooked broken noodles**
1   **tablespoon instant beef bouillon**
⅛   **teaspoon garlic powder**
¼   **teaspoon basil leaves, crushed**
1   **cup frozen mixed vegetables**

1. Spray hard plastic colander with vegetable cooking spray. Rest colander in microwave-safe dish.

2. Crumble ground beef into colander. Add onion.

3. Microwave on 100% power 2 minutes. Break up beef with chopper or fork. Microwave on 100% power another 1-2 minutes until meat is no longer pink.

4. In 2½ or 3 quart microwave-safe casserole, combine drained cooked meat mixture, water, noodles, bouillon, garlic powder and basil. Mix well.

5. Cover with lid or vented plastic wrap.

6. Microwave on 100% power 9-10 minutes or until noodles are just about tender, stirring once.

7. Stir in frozen vegetables.

8. Microwave, on 100% power uncovered, 2-3 minutes or until vegetables are tender.

BEEF CHOW MEIN FOR TWO

[Serves 2]

The microwave oven breathes new life into small quantity cooking. That's because the smaller the quantity of food, the faster it cooks in the microwave. Home cooked entrees like this chow mein idea are ready in minutes.

½   pound lean ground beef
1   cup diced celery
1   cup sliced fresh mushrooms
3   green onions, sliced
½   cup water
2   teaspoons cornstarch
1   teaspoon instant beef bouillon
2   teaspoons soy sauce
     Dash ground pepper

1. Crumble ground beef into 1 quart microwave-safe casserole.

2. Microwave, uncovered, on 100% power 3 to 4 minutes or until no longer pink, stirring once. Drain well.

3. Stir in celery, mushrooms and onions. Cover with casserole lid or vented plastic wrap.

4. Microwave on 100% power 5-6 minutes or until vegetables are tender.

5. Combine water, cornstarch, beef bouillon, soy sauce and pepper. Stir mixture into meat and vegetables.

6. Microwave, on 100% power uncovered, 2-3 minutes or until mixture boils and thickens, stirring once.

7. Serve over chow mein noodles or rice.

SESAME PORK

[Serves 6]

I would have to admit that I am partial to pork and to entrees prepared in the microwave oven. That's because I enjoy the flavor of pork and like quick cooking methods. With that criteria in mind, all that's needed is a flavorful recipe like this one.

1	tablespoon cornstarch
1	tablespoon brown sugar
¼	teaspoon ground ginger
¼	cup soy sauce
2	tablespoons white wine vinegar
1	tablespoon vegetable oil
1	pork tenderloin [¾ pound] trimmed and cut into 2 x ¼ inch strips [freeze for 1-2 hours for easier cutting]
¼	cup sliced green onions
2	cups frozen peas and carrots
1	tablespoon sesame seeds

1. In 2-quart microwave-safe casserole, combine cornstarch, brown sugar and ginger. Mix well.

2. Blend in soy sauce, vinegar and oil.

3. Add pork strips and green onions. Toss.

4. Microwave, uncovered, on 100% power 9-12 minutes or until pork is no longer pink and sauce is thickened, stirring 2 or 3 times.

5. Add peas and carrots.

6. Cover with lid or vented plastic wrap.

7. Microwave on 100% power 5-7 minutes, or until mixture is hot, stirring once.

8. Sprinkle with sesame seeds.

9. Serve.

DELUXE CREAMED POTATOES

[Serves 5 or 6]

It was during a phone conversation with my friend, Jean Hartman of Evansville, Indiana, that I learned about this potato recipe, a Hartman family favorite. Immediately, I knew I wanted the recipe. Jean willingly shared the entire process over the phone and within a few hours I'd tried this dish. Believe me, these potatoes are great and even more flavorful when reheated the next day. Jean says she sometimes adds cubes of turkey ham to create a main dish.

⅓   **cup water**
2   **tablespoons instant chicken bouillon**
6   **cups sliced potatoes**
¼   **cup chopped onion**
¾   **cup milk**
1   **tablespoon flour**
½   **teaspoon garlic salt**
¼   **teaspoon dill weed**
2   **tablespoon margarine**
¾   **cup light or regular sour cream**
½   **teaspoon prepared mustard**

1. In 3 quart microwave-safe casserole, combine water and chicken bouillon. Mix together.

2. Add potatoes and onion.

3. Cover with lid or vented plastic wrap. Microwave on 100% power 11-12 minutes until potatoes are tender, stirring once.

4. In 1 cup glass measurer, combine milk, flour, garlic salt and dill weed. Stir to evenly combine.

5. Add milk mixture to undrained cooked potatoes.

6. Microwave on 100% power 3-4 minutes until thickened, stirring once or twice.

7. Add margarine and sour cream that has been mixed with mustard. Stir gently to evenly combine.

8. Microwave an additional 2-3 minutes on 100% power until potatoes are very hot, stirring once.

ASPARAGUS AND CARROTS

[Serves 6-8]

Here in the Midwest, asparagus is traditionally a spring vegetable and carrots are harvested in the fall. However, both vegetables, especially carrots, are available all year long so you can prepare this wonderful vegetable combination.

2 **cups carrot slices**
2 **tablespoons water**
1 **pound fresh asparagus, cut into 1 inch pieces**
1 **tablespoon margarine**
¼ **teaspoon dried tarragon leaves, crushed**

1. Combine carrots and water in 2 quart microwave-safe casserole. Cover with casserole lid or vented plastic wrap.

2. Microwave on 100% power 5-6 minutes or until carrots are tender-crisp, stirring once. Add asparagus. Recover.

3. Microwave on 100% power 5-6 additional minutes or until asparagus is tender, stirring once. Drain.

4. Add margarine and tarragon; mix lightly.

PEA PODS WITH WATER CHESTNUTS

[Serves 4-6]

Bright green vegetables can often perk up menus that lack color. Pea pods will provide the needed color as well as delicious flavor, so try this recipe soon.

1 **pound [6 cups] fresh pea pods**
2 **tablespoons margarine or butter**
1 **tablespoon soy sauce**
1 **[8 ounce] can water chestnuts, drained**

1. Wash pea pods and snip off ends.

2. In 2 quart microwave-safe casserole, combine pea pods and margarine. Cover with lid or vented plastic wrap.

[continued]

PEA PODS WITH WATER CHESTNUTS

[continued]

3. Microwave on 100% power 5-6 minutes or until just about tender, stirring once.

4. Add soy sauce and chestnuts. Recover.

5. Microwave on 100% power 1-2 minutes until piping hot.

SESAME PEAS

[Serves 4]

For years, I've added a little chicken bouillon when cooking frozen peas. It just seems to give the peas a new depth of flavor. Add some sesame seeds and you have two reasons to remember this recipe when serving peas.

1	**[10 ounce] package frozen peas**
½	**teaspoon instant chicken bouillon**
¼	**teaspoon dry mustard**
¼	**teaspoon sugar**
1½	**teaspoons sesame seeds, toasted if desired**

1. Place peas and chicken bouillon in 1 quart microwave-safe casserole. Cover with lid or vented plastic wrap.

2. Microwave on 100% power 5-6 minutes or until just tender, stirring once.

3. Add mustard and sugar. Stir.

4. Sprinkle with sesame seeds.

5. Recover. Microwave on 100% power 1-2 minutes until hot.

PINEAPPLE SWEET POTATO BAKE

[Serves 4]

There's no need to save sweet potatoes for special meals when you can put together this make ahead vegetable idea in a matter of minutes. It's the perfect casserole accompaniment for ham. Complete the menu with an interesting green salad and cloverleaf rolls.

1   [23 ounce] can sweet potatoes, drained
3   tablespoons margarine or butter, softened
½   teaspoon salt
1   [8 ounce] can crushed pineapple, drained
⅓   cup orange juice
¼   cup brown sugar
¼   cup chopped pecans

1. In medium mixing bowl, mash drained sweet potatoes with margarine and salt.

2. Add drained pineapple, orange juice and brown sugar. Mix thoroughly.

3. Spoon into lightly greased 1 quart microwave-safe casserole; sprinkle with chopped pecans.

4. Cover and refrigerate until baking time, if desired.

5. Uncover.

6. Microwave on 80% power 10-12 minutes until thoroughly heated, rotating casserole once.

CRUMB-TOPPED TOMATOES

[Serves 5]

When the fresh tomatoes are in abundance, it's time to serve them hot as well as cold. This savory crumb mixture will provide a terrific topping for vine ripened tomatoes.

5   tomatoes
½   cup dry bread crumbs
2   tablespoons grated Parmesan cheese
¼   teaspoon garlic salt
¼   teaspoon dried basil leaves, crushed

[continued]

CRUMB-TOPPED TOMATOES [continued]

1. Cut tomatoes in half horizontally.

2. Arrange cut side up on microwave-safe serving plate.

3. In small bowl, combine bread crumbs, Parmesan cheese, garlic salt and basil leaves.

4. Sprinkle crumb mixture over tomato halves.

5. Microwave, uncovered, on 100% power 3-4 minutes or until heated.

LOVELY LIGHT CHEESE SAUCE

[Makes 1 cup]

Microwave ovens have made sauce making a reality for many cooks. Long gone is constant stirring and concern about lumps. Now, we can even cut the fat content. Hooray.

1   **cup water**
½   **cup instant non-fat dry milk powder**
1½ **tablespoons flour**
¼   **teaspoon salt**
     Pinch of white pepper
3   **drops of butter flavoring**
⅛   **teaspoon dry mustard**
¼   **cup shredded cheddar cheese**

1. In 1 quart microwave-safe measurer, combine water, milk powder and flour.

2. Microwave on 100% power 2-4 minutes, stirring with a whisk or fork every minute until thickened

3. Add salt, pepper, butter flavoring, dry mustard and cheese. Blend well.

4. Serve cheese sauce over vegetable of your choice.

GREAT GREEN BEANS

[Serves 4]

Here is a great way to show-off fresh green beans. It`really is worth a trip to the garden or your favorite Farmer's Market just to find fresh beans for this recipe. However, when necessary, frozen green beans are a good substitute.

½   cup water
3   cups cut fresh green beans [about 1 pound] or 3 cups loose pack frozen
    green beans
½   cup sliced green onions
1   cup sliced fresh mushrooms
2   tablespoons margarine
    Salt and pepper to taste

1. In 2 quart microwave-safe casserole, combine water and beans. Cover with lid or vented plastic wrap.

2. Microwave on 100% power 7-9 minutes or until beans are crisp-tender, stirring once. Let stand 1 minute. Drain.

3. In 1 quart microwave-safe bowl, combine onions, mushrooms and margarine.

4. Microwave on 100% power 2-3 minutes or until onions are crisp tender.

5. Stir onions and mushrooms into drained green beans

6. Season to taste with salt and pepper.

7. Microwave on 100% power 2-3 minutes or until thoroughly heated, rotating casserole once.

GARDEN PATCH COTTAGE CHEESE

[Serves 4-6]

Microwave cooking is an easy way to blanch just a few vegetables for creative uses. In this recipe, they give a "dressed up" look to everyday cottage cheese. It's both colorful and nutritionally sound.

1   **cup small broccoli flowerets**
1   **cup small cauliflower pieces**
1   **tablespoon water**
½   **cup shredded carrot**
1   **green onion, sliced**
½   **cup sliced radishes**
¼   **cup chopped green pepper**
1   **[12 ounce] carton cottage cheese [1 and ½ cups]**
¼   **teaspoon dill weed**
⅛   **teaspoon garlic powder**
⅛   **teaspoon dry mustard**
     Salad greens, if desired

1. Put broccoli, cauliflower, and water in 1 quart microwave- safe casserole. Cover with lid or vented plastic wrap.

2. Microwave on 100% power 3-4 minutes until crisp tender.

3. Drain and plunge into ice water until chilled. Drain again.

4. Combine carrot, green onion, radishes, green pepper, cottage cheese, dill weed, garlic powder and mustard in mixing bowl; mix lightly.

5. Stir in cooled vegetables.

6. Put into pretty dish, lined with salad greens if you wish.

7. Chill until serving time.

AMBROSIA-FILLED PINEAPPLE

[Serves 6-8]

"Pretty as a Picture" easily describes this fruit filled pineapple. This ambrosia would be delightful as a salad or dessert or could even double as both.

1 tablespoon sugar
1½ teaspoons cornstarch
½ cup orange juice
½ teaspoon grated orange rind
2 tablespoons shredded or flaked coconut
1 medium fresh pineapple
1 orange, peeled, sectioned and cut into chunks
1 banana, sliced
1 cup seedless red or green grapes
6 maraschino cherries

1. In 2 cup microwave-safe measurer, combine sugar, cornstarch and orange juice. Mix well.

2. Microwave, on 100% power, uncovered, 1-2 minutes or until thickened, stirring every 30 seconds. Stir in orange rind. Cool.

3. Microwave coconut in uncovered microwave-safe pie plate on 100% power 2-3 minutes or until lightly toasted, stirring every 30 seconds. Cool.

4. Cut pineapple in half lengthwise through leafy top. With grapefruit knife, cut around pineapple to remove fruit pulp, leaving ¼ inch rim. Remove core and cut pineapple into cubes.

5. Combine pineapple cubes with oranges, bananas, grapes and orange sauce.

6. Put fruit into pineapple shells. Sprinkle fruit with toasted coconut. Garnish with cherries.

7. Serve immediately or cover with plastic wrap and chill until serving time.

ROSY APPLE SALAD

[Serves 6]

I can remember the delicious red cinnamon apples my Mother created at our Howell family farm in southern Wisconsin. Here is an updated microwave method for transforming snowy white apples into bright red jewels. I like to use Jonathan apples just like Mother did.

1   **cup water**
½   **cup red cinnamon candies**
3   **medium apples, halved and cored**
1   **[3 ounce] package cream cheese**
1   **tablespoon lemon juice**
½   **cup chopped celery**
2   **tablespoons chopped pecans or walnuts**
    Lettuce leaves

1. Combine water and cinnamon candies in 2-quart microwave-safe casserole.

2. Microwave on 100% power 4-6 minutes or until candies dissolve, stirring once.

3. Add apples, cut-side-down. Microwave covered with lid or vented plastic wrap on 100% power 5-6 minutes or until apples are just about tender. Cool
and refrigerate.

4. In small microwave-safe dish, microwave cream cheese on 100% power for 15-30 seconds just until softened.

5. Mix in lemon juice, celery, and pecans.

6. At serving time, arrange drained, chilled apple halves on lettuce leaves.

7. Top with cream cheese mixture.

CUSTARD SAUCE WITH ANGEL FOOD CAKE

[Serves 8]

This rich and creamy custard sauce takes advantage of two heart smart ingredients; evaporated skim milk and frozen cholesterol-free egg product. It's a first class creation that's wonderful served over angel food cake with colorful fresh fruit.

1   cup evaporated skim milk
⅓   cup frozen cholesterol-free egg product, thawed
⅓   cup sugar
½   teaspoon vanilla
8   slices angel food cake
2   cups cut-up or whole fresh fruit like strawberries, peaches, blueberries and/or raspberries, etc.

1. In 2 quart microwave-safe measurer, microwave milk on 100% power for 1-2 minutes until hot.

2. In 1 cup glass measurer, beat egg product and sugar until well blended.

3. Gradually beat egg mixture into hot milk.

4. Microwave on 50% power 4-5 minute until thickened, stirring every minute.

5. Stir in vanilla.

6. Cover with plastic wrap. Cool. Store in the refrigerator.

7. At serving time, top slices of angel food cake with sauce and fruit.

MICHIGAN FRESH PEACH TOPPING

[Makes 3 cups]

Fresh peaches are show cased in this quick and easy sauce. Use the topping to create ice cream peach parfaits or sundaes. You'll find it's delicious over plain cake and meringues too.

½   cup sugar
2   teaspoons cornstarch
¾   cup orange juice
3-4 medium peaches, peeled, sliced

[continued]

MICHIGAN FRESH PEACH TOPPING

[continued]

1. In 1 quart microwave-safe measurer, combine sugar, cornstarch, and orange juice.

2. Microwave on 100% power 2-3 minutes, stirring every minute, until thickened.

3. Stir in peaches; cool.

4. Use with ice cream, plain cake or meringues.

RHUBARB STRAWBERRY SAUCE

[Serves 6]

Rhubarb and strawberries have been flavor pals for years. All the microwave cook needs is a plan like this recipe to create a delicious combination sauce.

2   **cups sliced fresh or frozen rhubarb**
¼   **cup water**
½   **cup sugar**
2   **cups sliced fresh strawberries**

1. Place rhubarb, sugar and water in 2 quart microwave-safe casserole.

2. Microwave on 100% power 5 to 7 minutes or until rhubarb begins to soften and break apart, stirring once or twice.

3. Add strawberries; stir gently.

4. Microwave on 100% power 1-2 minutes or until strawberries are warm and start to soften.

5. Serve warm or cold.

APPLE CRISP FOR TWO

[Serves 2]

Efficient cooks will pop this favorite dessert in the microwave oven as the main course is being prepared or even as the first course is eaten. Change the fruit to pears or peaches and you've created a brand new finale.

2	tablespoons quick-cooking or regular rolled oats
2	tablespoons brown sugar
1	tablespoon flour
⅛	teaspoon ground cinnamon
	Dash of ground nutmeg
	Dash of salt
1	tablespoon margarine or butter
2	cups peeled and sliced apples

1. In small mixing bowl, combine oats, brown sugar, flour, cinnamon, nutmeg and salt.

2. Cut in margarine with pastry blender or fork until crumbly; set aside.

3. Place apple slices in small microwave-safe casserole.

4. Top with rolled oat mixture.

5. Microwave on 100% power 3-5 minutes or until apples are tender, rotating casserole once.

6. Serve warm with frozen yogurt or ice cream, if desired

BAKED APPLE FOR ONE

[Serves 1]

It's hard to imagine an easier or quicker baked dessert than a delicious apple baked in a microwave oven. Remember, Rome Beauty apples are the first choice for baking apples; however, other types like Ida Red or Empire are popular too.

1	medium to large baking apple
1	tablespoon brown sugar
1½	teaspoons margarine or butter softened
	Dash of cinnamon

[continued]

BAKED APPLE FOR ONE [continued]

1. Core apple and slice the skin around the circumference ½ inch from the top.

2. Cream together the brown sugar, margarine and cinnamon.

3. Put the apple in small microwave-safe dish.

4. Fill the center of the apple with brown sugar mixture.Cover with waxed paper.

5. Microwave on 100% power 2 to 3 minutes, rotating the dish half way through cooking time.

6. Test the apple with a fork for tenderness to determine the cooking time.

BAKED CUSTARD

[Serves 6]

It's such fun to make an old fashioned recipe like this baked custard in the microwave oven. There are memories of how custard was traditionally baked in a pan of water and the realization that microwave methods are quicker and much easier.

2   **cups skim milk**
⅓   **cup sugar**
¾   **cup egg substitute or 3 eggs**
¼   **teaspoon salt**
1   **teaspoon vanilla**
    Ground nutmeg

1. Measure milk into 4 cup microwave-safe measurer.

2. Add sugar, eggs, salt and vanilla.

3. Beat with rotary beater until smooth.

4. Pour into six 5 ounce glass custard cups or coffee cups.

5. Sprinkle each one with nutmeg.

6. Microwave on 100% power for 4 minutes.

7. Rearrange cups and reduce power to 50%.

8. Microwave an additional 2-5 minutes or until custard is set.

9. Serve chilled.

TAPIOCA STRAWBERRY PARFAITS

[Serves 4-6]

For some folks, tapioca pudding brings to mind fond memories of foods eaten during childhood years. Today's updated version is heart healthy and cooked in the microwave. Add pretty fresh strawberry slices and these parfaits will be remembered by everyone.

2   cups skim milk
¼   cup sugar
2   tablespoons quick-cooking tapioca
⅛   teaspoon salt
¼   cup egg substitute or 1 egg
¼   teaspoon vanilla
⅛   teaspoon lemon extract
1-2 cups sliced fresh strawberries

1. Combine milk, sugar, tapioca, salt and egg substitute in 2 quart microwave-safe measurer.

2. Microwave on 100% power 6-8 minutes, stirring two or three times.

3. Stir in vanilla and lemon extract.

4. Cool.

5. In parfait glass, alternate layers of cooled pudding and sliced fresh strawberries

6. Garnish with a whole fresh strawberry, if desired.

7. Serve immediately or chill until serving time.

KIWI FRUIT TOPPING

[Makes 1 and 1/2 cups]

Kiwi fruit and apple juice team together as perfect partners in this lovely topping. Your friends and family members will be impressed by its simple beauty.

¼   cup sugar
2   teaspoons cornstarch
½   cup apple juice

[continued]

KIWI FRUIT TOPPING [continued]

¼ **teaspoon grated lemon peel**
3 **kiwi fruit, peeled and sliced**

1. In 2 cup microwave-safe measurer, combine sugar and cornstarch.

2. Stir in apple juice.

3. Microwave on 100% power 2-3 minutes, stirring every minute, until mixture thickens.

4. Stir in lemon peel and kiwi fruit; cool.

5. Serve at room temperature over angel food cake, meringues, pound cake, ice cream, etc.

CHOCOLATE PRALINE ICE CREAM TOPPING

[Makes 3 cups]

Chocoholics take note. This superb topping is designed for you. It's rich, creamy and the perfect way to celebrate a special occasion .

⅔ **cup margarine or butter**
⅔ **cup brown sugar**
1 **cup whipping cream**
1 **cup semi-sweet chocolate chips**
1 **cup pecan halves**

1. In 2 quart microwave-safe measurer, combine margarine, brown sugar and whipping cream.

2. Microwave on 100% power 4-5 minutes or until mixture comes to a full boil, stirring twice.

3. Add chocolate chips; stir.

4. Microwave on 100% power for 45-60 seconds until chocolate chips melt, stirring once.

5. Stir in pecans.

6. Serve warm over ice cream or other dessert.

7. Store covered in the refrigerator.

CRISPY POPS

[Makes 14]

Once you've melted marshmallows in the microwave oven, you'll never go back to the stovetop method. In double quick time, individual marshmallows are one giant puff. Just minutes later, the kids can help fill paper cups for this all time favorite sweet treat.

6   **cups crisp rice cereal**
1   **cup candy coated chocolate pieces**
¼   **cup margarine or butter**
1   **[10 and ½ ounce] package miniature marshmallows**
14 **[5 ounce] cold drink cups**
14 **wooden popsicle style sticks**

1. In large bowl, combine cereal and chocolate pieces.

2. In 2-quart microwave-safe measurer or bowl, place margarine and marshmallows.

3. Microwave on 100% power for 1-2 minutes, stirring after 1 minute. Beat until well blended.

4. Pour marshmallow mixture over cereal mixture; mix gently.

5. Fill each cup with cereal mixture; press lightly. Insert sticks; let cool completely.

6. To remove pops from paper cups, squeeze gently and pull on stick.

NOTE:

This cereal mixture can also be placed in a buttered 9 inch square pan and cut into squares to serve.

STRAWBERRY-RHUBARB JAM

[Makes 5 cups]

Strawberries and rhubarb have been flavor companions for years. Add the efficiency of the microwave oven and it's easy to modernize the entire jam making process.

1   **quart fresh strawberries**
2   **cups sliced rhubarb**
1   **[1 and ¾ ounce] package powdered fruit pectin**
4   **cups sugar**

[continued]

STRAWBERRY-RHUBARB JAM [continued]

1. Wash and hull strawberries.

2. Crush strawberries to make 2½ cups; combine with rhubarb in 2 quart microwave-safe measurer. Cover with vented plastic wrap.

3. Microwave on 100% power 5-6 minutes or until fruit is softened, stirring once. Stir in pectin.

4. Microwave, uncovered, on 100% power 3-4 minutes or until mixture boils, stirring once. Stir in sugar.

5. Microwave on 100% power 3-4 minutes or until mixture boils hard for at least 1 minute.

6. Pour into hot, sterilized jars.

7. Store in the refrigerator or freezer.

PINEAPPLE-KIWI JAM

[Makes 4½ cups]

Because small batches of jam and jelly cook quickly and efficiently in the microwave oven, they can be created whenever you're in the jam making mood. On a day when fuzzy kiwi fruit is on special at the grocery store, do try this innovative fruit combination.

4   kiwi, peeled, thinly sliced and halved
3   cups sugar
¼   cup lime juice
1   [8 ounce] can crushed pineapple, undrained
1   [3 ounce] package liquid fruit pectin
3   drops green food color

1. In 2 or 3-quart microwave-safe bowl, combine kiwi, sugar, lime juice and pineapple.

2. Microwave on 100% power for 10-16 minutes, or until mixture comes to full boil, stirring every 2 minutes.

3. Stir in liquid pectin. Microwave on 100% power 2-3 minutes or until mixture comes to full boil.

4. Microwave on 100% power for 1 minutes. Add food color.

5. Pour into clean jars.

6. Refrigerate 3 weeks or freeze up to 3 months.

MIXED NUT BRITTLE

[Makes about 1 pound]

If you've enjoyed making peanut brittle in the microwave oven, then I think you'll like this classy mixed nut brittle which follows the same easy procedure. It's a great way to use mixed nuts that are left after entertaining.

1   **cup sugar**
½   **cup light corn syrup**
1   **cup mixed nuts**
1   **teaspoon margarine or butter**
1   **teaspoon vanilla**
1   **teaspoon baking soda**

1. Line a baking sheet with foil. Spray with butter-flavored cooking spray or lightly butter.

2. In 2 quart microwave-safe measurer, combine sugar and corn syrup.

3. Microwave on 100% power 4 minutes, stirring after 2 minutes.

4. Add nuts; blend well.

5. Microwave on 100% power 3½ to 4½ minutes or until mixture is very light brown.

6. Stir in margarine and vanilla.

7. Microwave on 100% power 1 minute.

8. Add baking soda; stir quickly to blend.

9. Pour immediately onto buttered, foil-lined baking sheet, spread mixture quickly with wooden spoon.

10. Cool 30 minutes.

11. Break into pieces; store mix in an airtight container.

Food Gifts

Treasured gifts from the kitchen are gifts from the heart. Whether hours are spent baking the Candy Cane Coffee Cakes or just a few minutes, wedged into a busy schedule, to put together Sugar Free Spiced Tea Mix, these significant recipes are guaranteed to be welcome gifts.

Contents

CRANBERRY BREAD

[Makes 1 loaf]

This festive bread is a wonderful holiday gift from your kitchen. Baked loaves look so attractive when given in napkin lined wicker baskets.

2	cups flour
1	cup sugar
1½	teaspoons baking powder
½	teaspoon baking soda
1	teaspoon salt
¼	cup shortening
1	egg, beaten
¾	cup orange juice
1	tablespoon grated orange rind
1	cup fresh or frozen cranberries, chopped
½	cup chopped walnuts
1	tablespoon flour

1. In large mixing bowl, sift together 2 cups flour, sugar, baking powder, baking soda, and salt.

2. Cut in shortening until crumbs form, using a pastry blender or fork.

3. In small mixing bowl, combine the beaten egg, orange juice and orange rind. Add to crumb mixture all at once; stir until moistened.

4. Combine cranberries, walnuts and 1 tablespoon flour. Stir into batter.

5. Pour mixture into greased and parchment or waxed paper lined 8x4 inch baking pan.

6. Bake in preheated 350 degree oven 60-70 minutes, or until wooden pick inserted in center comes out clean.

7. Cool in pan on rack 10 minutes.

8. Remove from pan; cool on rack.

DRIED CHERRY APPLESAUCE BREAD

[Makes 1 loaf]

Dried cherries are coveted for both baking and snacking. So it's easy to understand why this special quick bread is a great gift from your kitchen.

1	**cup unsweetened or sweetened applesauce**
½	**cup margarine or butter, softened**
1	**cup sugar**
1	**egg**
2	**cups flour**
1	**teaspoon baking soda**
½	**teaspoon salt**
1	**teaspoon ground cinnamon**
1	**teaspoon ground nutmeg**
¼	**teaspoon ground cloves**
1	**cup dried cherries**
½	**cup chopped walnuts or pecans**

1. Heat applesauce in saucepan over low heat until hot.

2. In large mixing bowl, cream together margarine and sugar with electric mixer until light and fluffy. Beat in egg.

3. Sift together flour, baking soda, salt, cinnamon, nutmeg and cloves.

4. Alternately beat in dry ingredients and applesauce, beginning and ending with flour.

5. Fold in dried cherries and nuts.

6. Pour into well greased 8x4-inch baking pan.

7. Bake in preheated 325 degree oven for 60-70 minutes or until wooden pick comes out clean.

8. Cool in pan 10 minutes. Remove from pan. Cool.

Microwave

In step **1**, heat applesauce in microwave safe dish on full power for 2-3 minutes, stirring once.

Chocolate Pound Cake

When baking food gifts, it is thoughtful to remember dietary restrictions and promote healthy eating. One way to trim saturated fat and calories is to use unsweetened cocoa instead of chocolate products made with cocoa butter. This fine grained chocolate cake is an excellent example of a first class heart healthy food gift.

4	egg whites
1¾	cups sifted cake flour
2	teaspoons baking powder
¼	teaspoon salt
3	tablespoons unsweetened cocoa
¼	teaspoon ground cinnamon
¾	cup sugar
½	cup vegetable oil
½	cup evaporated skimmed milk
1	tablespoon vanilla

1. Beat egg whites until stiff. Set aside.

2. In large mixing bowl, sift together cake flour, baking powder, salt, cocoa, cinnamon and sugar.

3. Add oil, milk, and vanilla; with unwashed beaters of an electric mixer, beat at medium speed until well blended.

4. Add about one-third of egg whites; stir gently.

5. Fold in remaining egg whiles.

6. Pour batter in vegetable sprayed and parchment lined or floured 8x4-inch loaf pan.

7. Bake in preheated 350 degree oven for 45-55 minutes or until wooden pick inserted in center comes out clean.

8. Cool in pan 10 minutes; remove and cool on rack.

ALMOND TASSIES

[Makes 2 dozen]

A tassie can aptly be described as a tiny tender tart. This variation features toasted almonds and is just as delicious as its counterpart, the popular pecan tassie. Package baked tassies in paper cup lined, decorated egg cartons for a clever food gift from your kitchen.

1   **[3 ounce] package cream cheese, softened**
½   **cup margarine or butter, softened**
1   **cup flour**
1   **egg**
¾   **cup brown sugar**
1   **tablespoon margarine or butter, softened**
½   **teaspoon vanilla**
¼   **teaspoon almond extract**
   Dash salt
¾   **cup toasted slivered almonds, chopped**

1. In small mixing bowl, blend together the softened cream cheese and ½ cup margarine. Stir in flour. [This process can easily be done in a food processor]. Chill dough at least an hour.

2. Shape dough in 2 dozen 1-inch balls; place in ungreased 1¾-inch muffin pans.

3. Press dough evenly against bottom and sides of pan with fingertips or wooden "tart tamper", if available.

4. In 1 quart measurer, beat together egg, brown sugar, the 1 tablespoon margarine, vanilla, almond extract and dash of salt just until smooth.

5. Stir in chopped almonds.

6. Spoon mixture into pastry lined cups.

7. Bake in preheated 350 degree oven 20-25 minutes or until tassies are browned.

8. Cool in pans. Carefully run knife around outside to remove from pans.

HOLIDAY ICEBOX OATMEAL COOKIES

[Makes 3-4 dozen]

Several years ago, my friend, Blanche McCawley of Three Rivers, Michigan, shared this favorite Christmas cookie recipe with me. The ease of mixing, shaping, refrigerating and then baking the dough fits right into a busy holiday schedule.

1   **cup margarine or butter, softened**
1   **cup confectioners' sugar**
1   **teaspoon vanilla**
1½ **cups flour**
½   **teaspoon baking soda**
¼   **teaspoon salt**
1   **cup uncooked quick-cooking oatmeal**
     Red and/or green sugar crystals

1. In medium mixing bowl, cream margarine and confectioners' sugar until light and fluffy. Stir in vanilla.

2. Sift together flour, soda and salt.

3. Add dry ingredients to creamed mixture. Stir well.

4. Stir in oatmeal.

5. Chill dough until firm enough to form in rolls.

6. Shape into 4 rolls and roll in red or green sugar crystals.

7. Cover with foil or plastic wrap. Chill until firm.

8. Slice in ¾-inch slices and place on ungreased or parchment lined baking sheet.

9. Bake in preheated 325 degree oven about 15-20 minutes or until set and lightly browned.

COCONUT MACAROONS

[Makes 3-4 dozen]

These delicate macaroons look pretty when arranged on brightly colored plates for gift giving. Recipients will enjoy each mouth watering morsel.

[continued]

Coconut Macaroons [continued]

3   **egg whites**
1   **cup sugar**
1   **teaspoon vanilla**
½   **cup crushed saltine cracker crumbs**
1 ½ **cups flaked coconut**

1. Beat egg whites until foamy. Gradually add sugar and beat until stiff.

2. Beat in vanilla.

3. Fold cracker crumbs into egg whites. Gently fold in coconut.

4. Drop mixture by teaspoonful onto parchment lined or ungreased baking sheet.

5. Bake in preheated 325 degree oven for 20 minutes.

Toasted Pecans

[Makes 1 pound]

Ever since my friend, Alice Leach, shared this perfect gift giving recipe with me, these delicious pecans have been a favorite holiday gift from my kitchen. The ingredient list is so simple it could even be memorized. Best of all, here is a nonperishable food gift idea to send to far away family and friends.

1   **egg white**
1   **teaspoon sugar**
1   **teaspoon salt**
1   **teaspoon milk**
1   **teaspoon water**
1   **pound whole pecans**

1. In mixing bowl, gently beat egg white with rotary beater or whisk.

2. Add sugar, salt, milk, and water. Beat gently to combine ingredients.

3. Add pecans and stir to coat pecans with egg white ingredients.

4. Lightly oil a 10 ½ x 15-inch jelly roll pan. Transfer pecans to pan.

5. Bake in preheated 250 degree oven for 1 hour, stirring every 15 minutes. Cool.

6. Package in airtight containers for gift giving.

CANDY CANE COFFEE CAKES

[Makes 3 coffee cakes]

Food gifts are especially popular during the holiday gift giving season. Three festive yeast breads, shaped like candy canes, are the result of this efficient recipe that will make one coffee cake for your immediate family and two for gifts to extended family and friends.

2   **packages active dry yeast**
½   **cup warm water [105-115 degrees]**
1¼ **cups buttermilk**
½   **cup sugar**
½   **cup margarine or butter softened**
2   **eggs**
2   **teaspoons baking powder**
2   **teaspoons salt**
5½-6 **cups flour**
1½ **cups snipped dried apricots**
1½ **cups chopped drained maraschino cherries**
    Glaze, see recipe below

1. In large mixing bowl, dissolve yeast in warm water.

2. Add buttermilk, sugar, margarine, eggs, baking powder, salt and 2¼ cups flour. Beat on low speed of electric mixer, scraping bowl constantly, 30 seconds.

3. Beat on medium speed of mixer 2 more minutes, stirring bowl occasionally.

4. Stir in enough remaining flour to make dough easy to handle. [Dough will be soft and slightly sticky.]

5. Turn dough onto well-floured surface; knead until smooth and elastic, about 5 minutes.

6. Divide dough into three equal parts.

7. Roll each part into a rectangle 6x15 inches.

8. Place on ungreased or parchment lined cookie sheet.

9. Make 2-inch cuts on long sides of rectangle at 1/2 inch intervals.

10. In mixing bowl, combine apricots and cherries.

11. Spread a third of the fruit mixture lengthwise down center of each rectangle.

12. Crisscross strips over fruit mixture.

[continued]

CANDY CANE COFFEE CAKES [continued]

13. Stretch each rectangle to 22 inches, curve to form cane.

14. Cover with oiled plastic wrap.

15. Let rise in warm place until double. [Dough is ready if indentation remains when touched.]

16. Remove plastic wrap and bake in preheated 375 degree oven until golden brown, about 18-22 minutes.

17. Drizzle glaze over canes while warm.

18. Decorate with cherry halves or pieces, if desired.

GLAZE:

In small bowl, combine 2 cups confectioners sugar and 2 tablespoons water until of desired consistency.

SUGAR-FREE SPICED TEA MIX

[Makes 3 cups mix]

If a recipient on your gift giving list is on a sugar restricted diet or watching their sugar intake, this is the perfect food gift idea. It's fun to include a festive mug with the clearly labeled drink mix.

1   [3.3 ounce] jar sugar-free caffeine-free iced tea mix with lemon
2   [1.8 ounce] packages sugar-free orange breakfast drink mix
1   tablespoon plus 1 teaspoon ground cinnamon
2   teaspoons ground cloves

1. In large mixing bowl, combine iced tea mix, orange drink mix, cinnamon and cloves.

2. Whisk together to evenly combine.

3. Package in attractive airtight gift packages.

4. Attach these directions: Stir 1-2 teaspoons mix into 1 cup hot water.

"K" and "S" Trail Mix

[Makes 10 cups]

Our daughter, Sara, and her friend, Kris Land, have spent their college summers cooking for kids at Crystal Springs Camp, a United Methodist Camp near Dowagiac, Michigan. This is the mixture they created for hungry campers to enjoy during snack time.

5   cups honey-nut oat cereal
2   cups raisins
1   cup peanuts
1   cup sunflower seeds
1   cup semi-sweet chocolate chips

1. In large mixing bowl or large resealable plastic bag, combine cereal, raisins, peanuts, sunflower seeds and chocolate chips.

2. Stir or shake to evenly combine mixture.

3. Package in airtight container until snack time.

Dried Cherry Trail Mix

[Makes 7 cups]

My husband, George, once posed this question to me, "Where's that good snacking mix?" As far as I'm concerned that's reason enough to gather together these trail mix ingredients again and again. It' a great food fit for family and friends.

1   cup [6 ounces] dried cherries
2   cups crispy chex type cereal
½   cup banana chips
½   cup raisins
½   cup dried apples
½   cup semisweet chocolate chips
½   cup cashews
½   cup peanuts
½   cup sunflower seeds
½   cup coconut

[continued]

DRIED CHERRY TRAIL MIX [continued]

1. In large mixing bowl or resealable bag, combine dried cherries, chex cereal, banana chips, raisins, dried apples, chocolate chips, cashews, peanuts, sunflower seeds and coconut.

2. Mix carefully or shake the bag gently.

3. Package in airtight containers.

4. Share with treasured friends and family members.

CHICKEN NOODLE SOUP MIX

[Makes 1 cup]

For lots of folks, mixes are a favorite food gift idea. That's because non-perishable ingredients can be put together in minutes and the recipient can use when convenient. I like to slip this soup mix into a small cloth bag as described in *House Specialties* on page 274.

1 **cup uncooked fine egg noodles**
1 **tablespoon instant minced onion**
2½ **tablespoons chicken-flavored bouillon granules**
¼ **teaspoon pepper**
¼ **teaspoon thyme leaves**
⅛ **teaspoon celery seeds**
⅛ **teaspoon garlic powder**
1 **bay leaf**

1. In small plastic resealable plastic bag, combine noodles, onion, chicken bouillon, pepper, thyme, celery seeds, garlic powder and bay leaf.

2. Seal and label.

3. Put into festive cloth bag, if desired.

4. Attach directions.

DIRECTIONS FOR RECIPE GIFT CARD:

Combine soup mix, 8 cups water, and 1 diced carrot in Dutch oven. Bring to a boil; cover, reduce heat and simmer 15 minutes. Discard bay leaf. Stir in 3 cups cooked, diced chicken; simmer an additional 5 minutes.

GREAT GRANOLA

[Makes 4½ cups]

Homemade granola always tastes better to me than its commercial counterpart. This particular recipe has a low fat feature making it a heart smart high fiber food gift.

2   cups all bran cereal
1   cup old-fashioned or quick oats, uncooked
½   cup chopped walnuts
¼   cup sesame seeds
2   tablespoons honey, warmed
1   tablespoon vegetable oil
½   teaspoon cinnamon
1   cup raisins

1. In large mixing bowl, combine all bran cereal, oats, walnuts and sesame seeds.

2. Combine warmed honey, oil and cinnamon. Drizzle over dry mixture. Toss to moisten.

3. Lightly spray a 10½ x 15½ inch jelly roll pan with non stick cooking spray.

4. Pour mixture into prepared pan.

5. Bake in preheated 325 degree oven for 15-20 minutes, stirring once or twice.

6. Stir in raisins. Cool.

7. Package in airtight containers.

PINEAPPLE CHEESE SPREAD

[Makes 2¼ cups]

It takes just a few ingredients and a few minutes to whip together this appealing cheese spread. For gift giving, package cleverly in decorative jars and complete the gift with spreader and/or crackers.

2   [8 ounce] containers cream cheese with pineapple, softened
½   cup chopped pecans
¼   cup chopped red or green pepper
1   teaspoon finely chopped onion

[continued]

Pineapple Cheese Spread [continued]

1. In medium bowl, combine cream cheese, pecans, pepper and onion. Mix thoroughly.

2. Spoon mixture into decorative bowl, crock, jar or other containers. Cover; refrigerate to blend flavors.

3. Label with directions to keep refrigerated.

4. Attach spreader with pretty ribbons, if desired.

Michigan Mustard

[Makes 1½ cups]

If you save small jars like I do, you'll be glad that my friend, Judy Jolliffe, shared this mustard recipe with me. One tangy recipe will fill several jars that can be stored in the refrigerator until gift giving time. Add a bag of good quality pretzels to complete this great gift from your kitchen.

1 [3¼ ounce] can dry mustard [1 and ¼ cups]
1 cup white or garlic red wine vinegar
2 eggs
1 cup sugar
2 teaspoons cornstarch
  Dash of salt

1. In jar with tight fitting lid, combine mustard and vinegar.

2. Shake well to evenly combine.

3. Let stand in jar 24 hours, shaking several times.

4. Then, beat eggs, sugar, cornstarch and salt together in double boiler.

5. Add mustard mixture to egg mixture. Mix well.

6. Cook in double boiler until mixture is thickened and coats a metal spoon. Stir frequently with a wire whisk.

7. Pour into small jars.

8. Label with directions to keep refrigerated.

BRICKLE BARK

[Makes 1½ pounds]

Sweet tooth treats are popular food gifts from your kitchen. This "almost instant" crunchy candy is fun to give to family members and friends who are partial to chocolate.

1 **pound chocolate**
1 **[6 ounce] package almond brickle baking chips**

1. Melt chocolate over very low heat in a double boiler.

2. Stir in brickle baking chips.

3. Spread on waxed paper lined tray.

4. Refrigerate bark until set.

5. Break into pieces.

6. Package attractively for gift giving and store in cool, dry place.

Microwave

In step **1**, put chocolate in 2 quart microwave-safe measurer. Microwave on 50% power 4-6 minutes, stirring every minute until melted.

CHOCOLATE SPIDERS

[Makes 3 dozen]

Just the thought of Halloween reminds us of all the fun that always surrounds that holiday. Now cooks can add to the festive event by creating yummy chocolate treats.

1½ **cups semisweet chocolate morsels**
1 **[5 ounce] can chow mein noodles (3 cups)**
1 **cup salted peanuts**

1. Melt chocolate morsels in the top of a double boiler, stirring occasionally until chocolate is melted.

2. Add noodles and peanuts, stirring well to cover with melted chocolate.

3. Drop chocolate mixture by teaspoonfuls onto waxed paper-lined baking sheet or tray.

4. Refrigerate until set. Keep chilled until ready to serve to ghosts and goblins.

[continued]

CHOCOLATE SPIDERS [continued]

Microwave

> In step **2**, put semisweet chocolate morsels in 2 quart microwave-safe casserole. Microwave on 50% power 4-6 minutes, stirring every two minutes.

BEET PICKLES

[Makes 4 pints]

Because our son, Paul, is partial to beet pickles, he often makes a batch or two using this recipe. That assures mighty fine eating during the winter months and a jar or two to share with good friends.

4	**pounds small beets**
1	**quart vinegar**
1½	**cups sugar**
½	**teaspoon whole allspice**
1	**[2-inch] stick cinnamon**
1	**teaspoon whole cloves**

1. Cook the unpeeled beets in boiling water until tender when pierced with a fork.

2. Hold them under cold water and slip off the skins.

3. Halve or quarter the beets, if they are large.

4. In Dutch oven, combine vinegar, sugar, allspice, cinnamon and cloves.

5. Add the beets and bring mixture to a boil.

6. Reduce heat and simmer for 15 minutes.

7. Spoon beets into clean, hot, sterilized jars, fill with the cooking liquid, leaving ½ inch headspace. Adjust lids.

8. Process in boiling water bath 30 minutes.

9. Label and date before storing in a cool dry place.

Favorite Sweet Pickle Chunks

[Makes 5 pints]

In all honesty, I don't preserve as many pickles as I once did. However, when I do make them, this is my first choice for a wonderful crisp sweet pickle. Give them as a gift to your family first and then to friends.

10	**medium pickling cucumbers**
	Boiling water
8	**cups sugar**
1	**quart cider vinegar**
5	**tablespoons pickling salt**
2	**tablespoons mixed whole pickling spices**
2	**teaspoons celery seeds**

1. Wash cucumbers and cut off 1/16 inch from the blossom end.

2. Cover cucumbers with 4 quarts boiling water. Cover container. Let stand 12 hours. Drain. Repeat procedure 4 more times, by using fresh water and letting cucumbers and boiling water stand each time for 12 hours. Drain.

3. Slice cucumbers in ¼ to ½-inch slices.

4. Make syrup by combining sugar, vinegar and salt. Tie pickling spices and celery seeds in clean thin white cloth; add to syrup; heat to boiling. Pour over slices. Let stand 12 hours.

5. After 12 hours, drain the vinegar syrup, reheat to boiling and again pour over the cucumber slices. Let stand a day. Repeat this process 3 more days.

6. On the 4th day, pack slices in hot pint jars. Bring syrup to a boil; remove spices.

7. Pour hot syrup over slices in jars, leaving ½ inch head space; adjust lids.

8. Process in boiling water bath 5 minutes.

9. Remove from canner. Cool in draft free place.

BREAD AND BUTTER PICKLES

[Makes 8 pints]

Pickle connoisseurs rate these popular pickles as one of the best. In all honesty they really are very easy to make, especially if you use a food processor to slice the cucumbers and onions. Make several batches when pickling cucumbers are plentiful for great gifts any time of year.

4	**quarts thinly sliced cucumbers**
½	**cup pickling salt**
	Ice cubes
2	**quarts sliced onions**
1	**quart cider vinegar**
4	**cups sugar**
1	**tablespoon celery seeds**
2	**tablespoons mustard seeds**
1	**tablespoon ground ginger**
1	**teaspoon ground turmeric**
½	**teaspoon white pepper**

1. Gently stir salt into thinly sliced cucumbers.

2. Cover with ice cubes; let stand 2-3 hours or until cucumbers are crisp and cold. Add more ice, if it melts.

3. Drain; add onions.

4. In large saucepan, combine vinegar, sugar, celery seeds, mustard seeds, ginger, turmeric, and pepper. Bring mixture to a boil, boil 10 minutes.

5. Add cucumber and onion slices and bring to a boiling point.

6. Pack loosely at once in hot jars; adjust lids.

7. Process in boiling water bath 15 minutes. Remove jars from canner and cool in draft free place.

RASPBERRY VINEGAR

[Makes 1 pint]

It's such fun to make flavored vinegars like this red raspberry version. Attractively labeled, filled bottles of finished vinegar can then be easily stored until the perfect gift giving moment. If time permits, attach directions for Raspberry Vinaigrette to each bottle.

1   **cup fresh red raspberries**
1½   **cups distilled white vinegar**

1. Bruise the raspberries with the back of a spoon.

2. Place raspberries in sterilized pint jar.

3. Heat vinegar to just below the boiling point.

4. Fill jar with vinegar and cap tightly.

5. Allow to stand in dark cool place 2 to 3 weeks.

6. Strain vinegar, discarding fruit.

7. Pour into a clean sterilized jar. Cap with non-metal lid.

8. Label clearly.

9. Attach directions for raspberry vinaigrette, if desired.

RASPBERRY VINAIGRETTE

[Makes 1 cup]

½   **cup raspberry vinegar**
½   **cup vegetable oil**
2   **teaspoons Dijon prepared mustard**
1   **tablespoon honey**
¼   **teaspoon salt**
⅛   **teaspoon pepper.**

1. In jar with tight fitting lid, combine vinegar, oil, mustard, honey, salt and pepper.

2. Cover and shake vigorously.

3. Chill to blend flavors.

4. Shake again before serving with mixed green salads.

Special Additions

Here are some ideas designed to help cooks use and enjoy the simply significant recipes shared in this collection.

You will find step-by-step instructions for making Yogurt Cheese. Use this delicious lowfat cheese for recipes in this book as well as in your everyday cooking.

Whenever you are searching for menu suggestions, they are easily found in this chapter as well as a very complete cross-referenced index. Note too, the "Cooking With Less" index.

Contents

LET'S MAKE YOGURT CHEESE

Yogurt Cheese has the whey from the yogurt drained away yielding a pure, soft cheese that spreads easily and resembles the consistency of cream cheese.

There are several quick and easy ways to transform plain yogurt or flavored yogurts such as vanilla or lemon into Yogurt Cheese. The flavored yogurts lose almost all of the sweetener calories in the whey, but the cheese still has a sweet taste. Because of this, yogurt cheese made from plain yogurt or flavored yogurt has about the same calorie content.

[**One ounce of yogurt yields approximately 1/2 ounce of yogurt cheese or in other words 16 ounces of yogurt yields 8 ounces of yogurt cheese.**]

JUST FOLLOW THESE STEPS TO CREATE WONDERFUL YOGURT CHEESE:

1. Line a colander with 4 layers of white paper towel, double thickness of coffee filters or several layers of cheesecloth.
2. Place desired amount of yogurt directly on paper towel, coffee filter or cheesecloth.
3. Cover with 3 or 4 more paper towels, pressing towels down into yogurt.
4. Place colander in a dish or pan to catch liquid.
5. Refrigerate 8-24 hours, depending on consistency desired.
6. Remove cheese from towels.
7. Yogurt Cheese may be stored, covered, in the refrigerator up to two weeks.

Use yogurt that does not contain gelatin as gelatin prevents the whey from separating from the yogurt.

Yogurt Cheese can be used instead of cream cheese, sour cream or mayonnaise in many of your favorite recipes. When using yogurt cheese in place of mayonnaise, you can retain the mayonnaise flavor by combining 2 parts Yogurt Cheese with 1 part mayonnaise.

The recipes in this cookbook that refer to Yogurt Cheese are:
Mini Rice Cake Morsels, page 19
Creamy Fruit Dip, page 20
Strawberry Lemon Cheesecake, page 208

Be creative, experiment with using Yogurt Cheese the next time you want to cut fat content and calories from a recipe that calls for cream cheese, sour cream or mayonnaise.

Menu Suggestions

This collection of significant recipes is designed to be used not only to prepare individual recipes, but to create entire menus. Keep in mind that variety in color, flavor, shape, temperature and texture are the cornerstones to interesting menus.

Then too, it's important to review the amount of time, energy and skill it takes to complete each recipe. That way you aren't exhausted when the menu is served.

Here are some menu ideas:

Healthy Breakfast
Orange Juice
Happy Heart Strata
Oatmeal Applesauce Muffins

Make Ahead Breakfast
Frozen Fruit Cups
Praline French Toast
Sausage Links

Lunch for Two
Deli Ham Melts
Orange Salad with Honey Dressing
Spanish Peanut Drop Cookie

Soup and Salad Luncheon
Salmon Corn Chowder
Greek Style Salad
Honey Whole Wheat Bread
Fresh Strawberry Sauce

Brunch For A Bunch
Sparkling Apple Cider
Fruit Fiesta
Hash Brown Quiche
Dawn's Lovely Yeast Coffee Cake

Candlelight Dinner For Two
Lamb Chops For Two
Garden Rice Pilaf
Broccoli Polonaise
Pear and Grape Salad
Dilly Spoon Rolls
Hidden Treasure Meringues

Heart Smart Cook-Out
Barbecued Halibut
Grilled Marinated Vegetables
Fruit and Pasta Salad
Heart Smart Hot Bread
Chocolate Pound Cake

Family Gathering Dinner
Golden Chicken Rolls
Celebration Rice
Asparagus and Carrots
Cranberry Gelatin Salad
Parmesan French Bread
Rainbow Sherbet Freeze

Microwave Dinner For Four
Mexican Chicken Breasts
Deluxe Creamed Potatoes
Sesame Peas
Rosy Apple Salad
Tapioca Strawberry Parfaits

[continued]

MENU SUGGESTIONS [continued]

Pot Luck Menu Ideas
Broccoli Ham Au Gratin
Turkey Tetrazzini
Brussels sprouts En Casserole
Cheesy Baked Corn
Marinated Zucchini
Tabbouleh
Cheesecake Bars

Family Pleasing Supper
Popover Pizza Casserole
Herbed Apple Salad
Old Fashioned Cole Slaw
Bread and Butter Pickles
Mary's Marbled Cupcakes

Dinner For Eight
Berry Barbecued Pork Roast
Do-Ahead Mashed Potatoes
Asparagus with Toasted Pecans
Molded Peach Melba Delight
Orange Marble Freeze

Lake Michigan Picnic
Picnic Tortilla Roll-Ups
Colorful Marinated Asparagus
Yogurt Ambrosia
"K" and "S" Trail Mix
Peanut Butter cookies

Holiday Hors d'oeuvre Party
Raspberry Cooler
Jan's Cheese Tarts
Honey Glazed Chicken Wings
Chutney Spread
Dilled Vegetable Sticks
Curried Munch Mix
Almond Tassies

Tailgate Gathering
Dried Cherry Trail Mix
Roast Beef Barbecues
Michigan Garden Relish
Herbed Apple Salad
Marble Brownies

Casual Supper For Friends
Turkey Black Bean Chili
Oatmeal Squash Bread
Apple Yum Yum Salad
Beet Pickles
Soft Gingerbread with Lemon Sauce

INDEX

INDEX COOKING WITH LESS

Recipes highlighted with this symbol contain less fat, less salt, or less sugar.

ORDER FORMS

House Specialties
P.O. Box 242
Ada, MI 49301

Please send _____ copies of *Even More House Specialties* at $14.95 per copy, plus $2.50 for postage and handling. For Michigan delivery add $.60 tax per book.

Why not complete your set and order *House Specialties* and *More House Specialties*!

Please send _____ copies of *House Specialties* at $14.95 per copy, plus $2.50 for postage and handling. For Michigan delivery add $.60 tax per book.

Please send _____ copies of *More House Specialties* at $14.95 per copy, plus $2.50 for postage and handling. For Michigan delivery add $.60 tax per book.

Make checks payable to **House Specialties**.

Name

Address

City   State   Zip

Special Savings on Books mailed to one address; Order two books and pay only $4.00 postage. Order three or more books sent to one address and receive **Free** Shipping via UPS.

ORDER FORMS

House Specialties
P.O. Box 242
Ada, MI 49301

Please send _____ copies of *Even More House Specialties* at $14.95 per copy, plus $2.50 for postage and handling. For Michigan delivery add $.60 tax per book.

Why not complete your set and order *House Specialties* and *More House Specialties*!

Please send _____ copies of *House Specialties* at $14.95 per copy, plus $2.50 for postage and handling. For Michigan delivery add $.60 tax per book.

Please send _____ copies of *More House Specialties* at $14.95 per copy, plus $2.50 for postage and handling. For Michigan delivery add $.60 tax per book.

Make checks payable to **House Specialties**.

Name

Address

City   State   Zip

Special Savings on Books mailed to one address; Order two books and pay only $4.00 postage. Order three or more books sent to one address and receive **Free** Shipping via UPS.

Please Note

All copies will be sent to the same address unless otherwise specified. If you wish one or any number of books sent as gifts, furnish a list of names and addresses of recipients. If you wish to enclose your own gift card with each book, please write name of recipient on outside of the envelope, enclose with order, and we will include it with your gift.

Please Note

All copies will be sent to the same address unless otherwise specified. If you wish one or any number of books sent as gifts, furnish a list of names and addresses of recipients. If you wish to enclose your own gift card with each book, please write name of recipient on outside of the envelope, enclose with order, and we will include it with your gift.